READ COMPREHENSION

2ND GRADE

SUCCESS WORKBOOK

This Book Belongs To:

POLYMATH Panda

ISBN: 978-1-953149-57-2

Copyright © 2024 by Polymath Panda

No part of this publication may be reproduced, distributed, or transmitted in any form or by any means, including photocopying, recording, or other electronic or mechanical methods, without the prior written permission of the publisher, except in the case of brief quotations embodied in critical reviews and certain other noncommercial uses permitted by copyright law.

Table of Contents

Unit 1: Phonics and Word Recognition .... **Pages** 5-24, **Activities** 1- 20
Common Core Standards:
RF.2.3, RF.2.3a, RF.2.3b, RF.2.3c, RF.2.3d, RF.2.3e

Unit 2: Reading Fluency .... **Pages** 25-44, **Activities** 21-40
Common Core Standards:
L.2.2, L.2.4a, RF.2.3, RF.2.3c, RF.2.3d, RF.2.4, RF.2.4a, RF.2.4b,
RF.2.4c, RI.2.1, RI.2.2, RL.2.4, RL.2.6, RL.2.10, SL.2.1, SL.2.2, SL.2.6

Unit 3: Informational Text .... **Pages** 45-64, **Activities** 41-60
Common Core Standards:
L.2.4, L.2.5, RI.2.1, RI.2.2, RI.2.3, RI.2.4, RI.2.5, RI.2.6, RI.2.7, RI.2.8,
RL.2.1, RL.2.2, RL.2.3, RL.2.4, RL.2.5, RL.2.6, RL.2.7, RL.2.9, SL.2.1

Unit 4: Literature .... **Pages** 65-84, **Activities** 61-80
Common Core Standards:
L.2.1d, L.2.1e, L.2.3a, L.2.4a, L.2.4c, L.2.4d, L.2.5, L.2.5a, L.2.5b, L.2.6,
RI.2.4, SL.2.2, SL.2.6

Unit 5: Vocabulary and Language .... **Pages** 85-104, **Activities** 81-100
Common Core Standards:
L.2.1e, L.2.1f, L.2.2a, L.2.2b, L.2.2c, L.2.4a, L.2.5a, L.2.6, RI.2.1, RI.2.3,
RI.2.5, RI.2.6, RL.2.1, W.2.1, W.2.2, W.2.3, W.2.5, W.2.7, W.2.8

Remember to:

- Carefully read the instructions for each activity.
- Color all the fun doodles on each page.
- Take your time and do your best.
- Check your answers when you're done.
- Ask for help if you need it.
- Use your creativity in writing and drawing.
- Have tons of fun!

Welcome

Hello Amazing Reading Teammate,

We're thrilled to have your young reader join us on this exciting journey through the world of reading. Our goal? To make this voyage educational and incredibly fun!

Your child will explore essential reading skills, from phonics to understanding various text types. We've filled this workbook with interactive activities, challenging puzzles, and engaging exercises designed to keep their enthusiasm high and reinforce their reading skills.

We encourage you to dive into this workbook together, discuss the fascinating stories, and celebrate each reading milestone. Remember, every step on the reading path is an opportunity for discovery, laughter, and learning.

Thank you for joining us on this exhilarating adventure. We're excited to help foster a lifelong love of reading in your child.

Happy Reading Adventures!

Warm regards,

Polymath Panda

10 Bonus Audio Stories!

- **A Treasure Trove of Stories:** Explore 10 unique tales full of adventure, humor, and wonder, from magical gardens to deep-sea explorations.
- **Listen Along:** Enjoy each story with an accompanying audio version, perfect for immersive storytimes or following along.
- **Learning is Fun:** Aligned with 2nd grade Common Core Standards, our stories enhance key skills like reading comprehension, creative writing, and critical thinking, making learning enjoyable.

QR Code in the Back of the Book

Activity 1 — Unit 1 — CCSS: RF.2.3

Alphabet Soup

Instructions

Look for words that start with each letter Timmy stirs into his pot. Can you match a word for every letter on the spoons in the soup picture? Write them down and see how many you can find.

Timmy was making a special alphabet soup. He added the letter 'B,' and a bright butterfly appeared. Then, he added 'C,' and a cute cat jumped into the room.

Next, Timmy added 'D,' and a dog barked outside. He added 'F,' and a fish splashed in his fishbowl.

Then, he added 'G,' and a green plant started to grow. Adding 'H' made a funny hat fall on his head. Timmy added 'S' and a shiny starfish swam around the pot, making the soup sparkle.

After that, he added 'L,' and a bright light lit up the room. With 'M,' a soft melody played, and with 'P,' a pumpkin appeared.

Adding 'R' made a small robot roll around. Finally, with 'T,' a tiny turtle crawled into the soup, making it smell yummy.

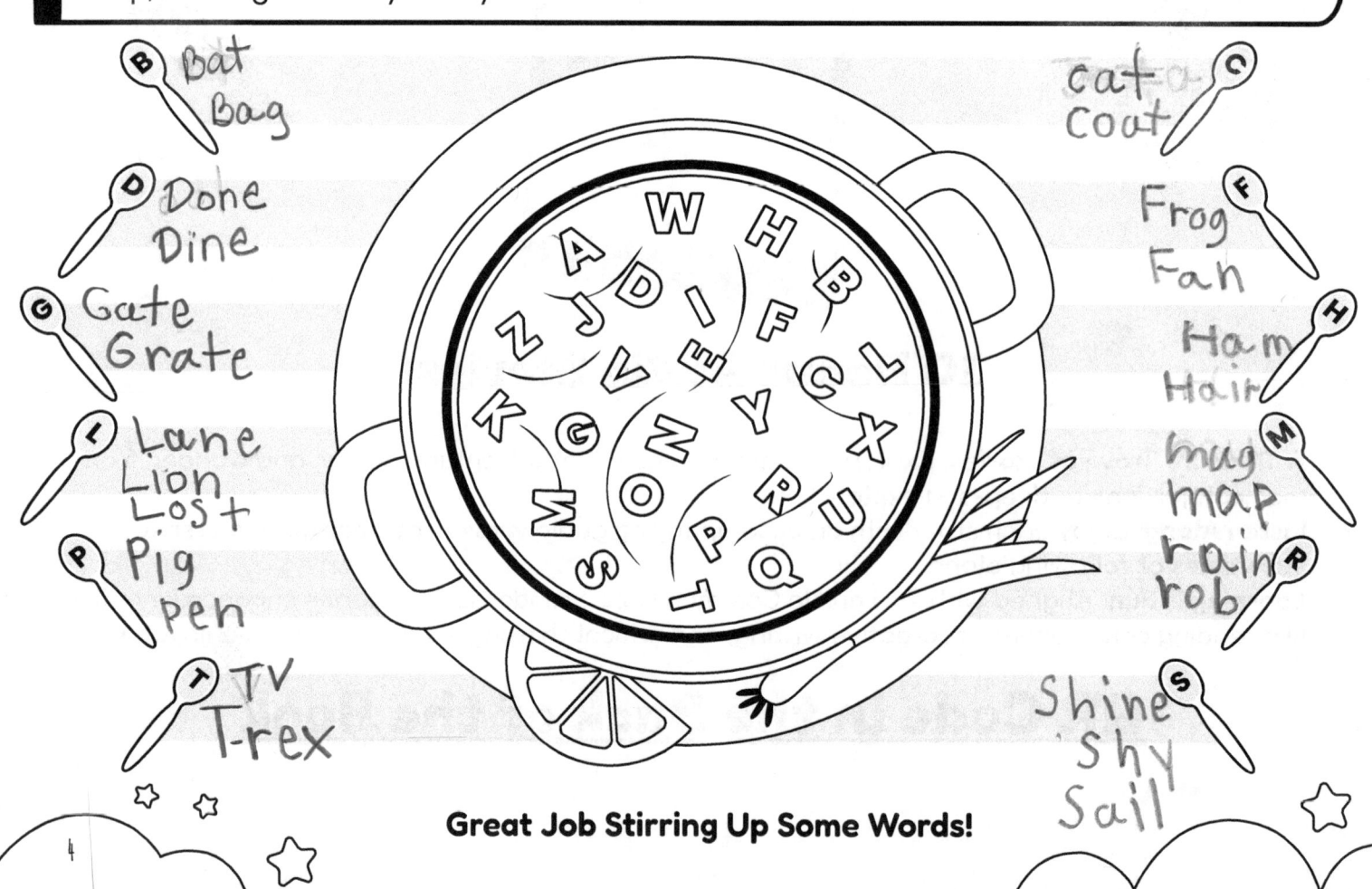

B - Bat, Bag
C - Cat, Coat
D - Done, Dine
F - Frog, Fan
G - Gate, Grate
H - Ham, Hair
L - Lane, Lion, Lost
M - mug, map
P - Pig, Pen
R - rain, rob
T - TV, T-rex
S - Shine, Shy, Sail

Great Job Stirring Up Some Words!

Activity 2 — **Unit 1** — CCSS: RF.2.3a

Word Family Tree

Discover words that belong to the same family!

Instructions

1. Start by reading the story about the Wordland forest. Look for words that end with "-at," "-in," or "-og."
2. As you read, find words that belong to each word family. Each tree represents a different family.
3. Write the words you find on the correct tree.

For example, write words that end in "-at" on the tree with "-at" at its base.

In the Wordland forest, a playful cat loved to bat at floating leaves. The cat wore a funny hat and often sat on a flat mat under a shady tree.

Nearby, twin mice named Min and Lin would spin in the wind, making everyone grin. They enjoyed playing in the sun.

Deep in the forest, near a foggy bog, lived a cheerful frog. The frog liked to jump over a big log and enjoyed a good jog around the bog.

-at

-in

-og

Fantastic Job!

Activity 3 — Unit 1 — CCSS: RF.2.3d

Sight Word Search

Find the hidden sight words!

Words

Always	Fast	Found	These	~~Us~~	Wash	Work
Around	First	Gave	Those	Use	Which	Would
Because	Five	Their	Upon	~~Very~~	Wish	Your

```
F  W  A  W  U  W  B  I  C  V  E  R  Y  G  A
O  I  L  Q  H  Q  L  D  K  M  M  T  E  H  V
U  S  O  I  M  E  H  N  B  E  C  A  U  S  E
N  H  C  E  A  G  S  U  I  P  T  W  U  A  R
D  H  R  V  N  L  W  O  R  K  H  A  S  W  U
Q  H  I  A  J  B  W  R  H  Q  E  V  E  T  O
W  O  E  G  N  O  F  A  C  T  S  V  B  S  Y
Q  N  H  L  U  Y  M  R  Y  P  E  S  O  R  W
T  T  T  L  E  W  U  F  A  S  T  E  V  I  F
M  U  D  E  F  I  S  U  J  S  E  I  X  F  X
```

Well Done! Sight Words Help You Read Faster

Activity 4 — **Unit 1** — CCSS: RF.2.3e

Syllable Split

Tim's Zoo Adventure

Tim went to the zoo with his family. They saw a colorful **butterfly** fluttering and a big **elephant** splashing water.

Next, they visited the **computer** room where they learned about animals. In the **garden**, they saw a **tiger** walking. Tim enjoyed eating a **chocolate** ice cream while watching playful **dolphins**.

He was amazed by the long **caterpillar** on a leaf and wished he could ride a **bicycle** around the zoo. Before leaving, Tim bought a **banana** for a snack. As they walked out, Tim felt happy and excited about his adventurous day.

He couldn't wait to come back and see more animals with his family.

Instructions

In the story below, you'll find words in bold. Split these words into syllables and write them in the boxes. Say each syllable out loud to hear the word parts!

1. **Butterfly** — But | ter | fly
2. **Elephant** — El | ep | phant
3. **Computer** — Com | pu | ter
4. **Garden** — Gar | den
5. **Chocolate** — Choc | ol | ate
6. **Tiger** — Ti | ger
7. **Dolphin** — Dol | phin
8. **Caterpillar** — Cat | er | Pill | ar
9. **Bicycle** — Bic | cy | cle
10. **Banana** — Ban | na | na

Fantastic Job!

Activity 5 — Unit 1 — CCSS: RF.2.3

Blend Buddies

Instructions
1. Look at the beginning blends on the left.
2. Match the blends to the words on the right.
3. Say each word out loud after you match them!

Blend List
1. bl-
2. tr-
3. gr-
4. cl-
5. fl-
6. dr-
7. pr-
8. st-
9. pl-
10. br-

Words to Match
- ⑥ drum
- ⑧ star
- ① blue
- ③ grass
- ② tree
- ⑩ bread
- ⑨ plane
- ⑤ flower
- ④ clap
- ⑦ prize

You Did An Excellent Job

Activity 6 — Unit 1 — CCSS: RF.2.3

Digraph Detective

Instructions

1. While reading the story, circle the digraphs in each bold word.
2. For each digraph you find, write two more words that contain the same digraph.

Example:
For the word **"chair"**, you would circle **"ch"** in the story. Can you think of two more words that have the **"ch"** digraph? Write them on the lines provided or use the word bank for ideas.

Shawn the Sheep's Day Out

In a sunny **town**, there was a talking **chair** named Charlie. Charlie had a friend, a **sheep** named Shawn.

One day, Shawn and Charlie crossed a wooden **bridge** to find new friends. They saw a big **whale** swimming in the river and heard a **thing** go 'buzz' in the trees.

They played until it was getting **long** into the evening. Then, they found a funny book about a **boot** that could dance. They read the **book** under a tall tree and laughed together.

It was a day full of fun and new words!

1. Town (Ow)   owl   grow
2. Chair (Ch)   Chain   Church
3. Sheep (Sh)   Shell   she
4. Bridge (Dg) Budget   Judge
5. Whale (Wh)   What   why
6. Long (Ng)   ring   King
7. Book (Oo)   Boot   Boom
8. Boot (Oo)   Dool   food
9. Thing (Th)   Think   That

Fantastic Job!

Activity 7 **Unit 1** **CCSS: RF.2.3b**

Long Vowel Voyage

Instructions
1. **Read the Story:** As you read, look for words with long vowel sounds.
2. **Circle Long Vowel Words:** Circle the words in the story that have long vowel sounds.
3. **Color the Bubbles:** After reading the story, color the bubble next to the words in the list according to the color key.

The Colorful Vowel Adventure

Lily and her friends were excited to go on an adventure. They started by climbing a tall tree, where they saw a beautiful rainbow in the sky. The rainbow was bright and colorful, stretching across the horizon.

After climbing down, they took their bikes to explore the forest. They rode past a quiet lake, where they saw some ducks floating near a small boat. They stopped to skip stones across the water, watching them bounce.

As they continued their journey, they found a kite stuck in a branch. They untangled it and flew it high in the sky. It was so much fun to see the kite soar. The friends later reached a picnic spot, where a large table was set with a delicious cake. They sat down to enjoy the cake and talk about their adventure.

Before heading home, they stopped to admire the lush garden and spotted a mule grazing nearby. It was a fantastic day filled with wonderful sights and experiences.

Color Key
A = Red   **E** = Green   **I** = Light Blue   **O** = Yellow   **U** = Purple

1. Tree
2. Lake
3. Kite
4. Boat
5. Cake

6. Rainbow
7. Table
8. Bike
9. Stone
10. Mule

Hooray! You Did It.

Activity 8 — **Unit 1** — CCSS: RF.2.3b

Short Vowel Adventure!

Instructions

1. Read about Tim's birthday party and the words he found on the balloons.
2. Find words in the story that have short vowel sounds, like "cat" and "bed."
3. Use each word to write a creative sentence. Try to use your imagination to make the sentences fun!

Example:
For the word "cat," you could write a sentence like: "The small cat hid under the chair during Tim's loud birthday party."

Tim's Birthday Party

Tim had the best birthday party ever. His mom hid words on balloons in the garden, and Tim and his friends had to find them. Some balloons had words with short vowel sounds, like "cat," "bed," "fish," and "pot." Others had words with long vowel sounds, like "bike" and "home." Tim's job was to find the balloons with short vowel words and use them to create sentences.

Tim's friends helped him find the balloons. They laughed and played games while looking around. They found balloons under the table, on the swing set, and even in the bushes. The friends shared the words they found and helped each other make funny sentences.

Everyone had a great time at Tim's birthday party, and they learned a lot about vowels and words.

1. Cat

_____

2. Bed

_____

3. Fish

_____

4. Pot

_____

5. Sun

_____

Your Hard Work Paid Off- Celebrate!

Activity 9 — Unit 1 — CCSS: RF.2.3c

Magic E Mystery

Instructions
1. **Look at the Words:** Find the words that Ellie the Magic Wand touches.
2. **Write the New Word:** Add an "e" to each word to create a new one. Write the new word in the box.
3. **Draw a Picture:** Illustrate how each word changes with the magic "e."

The Magic E Wand

Once in a small town, there was a curious wand named Ellie. She wasn't an ordinary wand—she was a "Magic E Wand." Whatever she touched, she added an "e" and transformed it magically! One sunny day, Ellie decided to demonstrate her power.

She first met a young boy with a plain, wooden cap. With a gentle tap, it became a marvelous cape! The boy danced around in delight.

Next, Ellie found a baker with a flat, unrisen mat of dough. A quick swish, and it was a fluffy, tasty mate! The baker beamed, serving his new treat.

Ellie loved showing how adding an "e" can magically change words. She continued her journey, eager to help more friends discover the magic of words.

1. Kit
2. Pin
3. Can
4. Hop
5. Cub

Activity 10 — **Unit 1** — CCSS: RF.2.3

R-Controlled Rockstars

Instructions
Read the story, then underline the r-controlled vowels in the word bank. Next, write each word under the correct band member according to their r-controlled sound, and finally, circle or star your favorite word!

Rock and Roll with R-Controlled

In the lively town of Harmonia, the annual music festival was everyone's favorite event. This year, the **'R-Controlled Rockstars'** were set to perform. Each band member was famous for using words with a special r-controlled sound in their songs. Arnie sang with **'ar'** sounds, Iris used **'ir'** sounds, Orlando rocked the **'or'** sounds, Ursula loved the **'ur'** sounds, and Eric was all about **'er'** sounds. Their music filled the air, and each song told a story using words with these unique sounds.

Words

car	star	farm	stir	bird	third	form	her
storm	port	turn	burn	curl	fern	better	

Arnie (ar)   **Iris (ir)**   **Ursula (ur)**   **Orlando (or)**   **Eric (er)**

_____ _____ _____ _____ _____

_____ _____ _____ _____ _____

_____ _____ _____ _____ _____

Activity 11 — Unit 1 — CCSS: RF.2.3c

Prefix Playhouse

Instructions

Read the story to understand the context and find words with prefixes. Then, draw lines to match the base words to the correct prefixes. Create new words by adding the prefixes to the base words. Finally, write the new words under each base word.

The Magic of Prefixes!

Once upon a time, in a magical world of words, there was a famous stage known as the Prefix Playhouse. Here, words would come alive with new meanings when they put on special prefix costumes. Every year, a grand performance was held where simple words transformed into exciting new characters!

One day, a cheerful word put on the "un-" costume and suddenly became the opposite of itself. Another word, eager to try again, put on the "re-" costume and was ready for a second chance. One word even showed how it felt when it wasn't pleased by changing into "dis-". Another gave everyone a sneak peek of what was to come by wearing the "pre-" costume.

The grand performance ended with all the transformed words taking a bow, and the crowd cheered, thrilled by the magical show of prefixes and their power to create new meanings. The Prefix Playhouse was a wonderful place where words and their playful transformations brought joy and learning to everyone.

Words

1. Happy
2. Do
3. Like
4. View
5. Play

Prefixes

- re-
- un-
- dis-
- pre-
- mis-

Superb Effort—keep It Up!

Activity 12　　　　　　　　　**Unit 1**　　　　　　　　**CCSS: RF.2.3d**

Suffix Splash

Instructions

1. Read the story to understand the context and find words with suffixes.
2. Fill in the boxes with the correct suffixes to create new words.
3. Write the new words under each base word.

Adventures in Wordland's Suffix Splash

In the colorful world of Wordland, there was a magical pool known as the Suffix Splash. Whenever someone jumped into the pool with a word, that word would gain a special suffix and come to life with a new meaning. One sunny day, five friends decided to take a dip in the Suffix Splash with their favorite words: joy, hope, play, rain, and wonder. They were excited to see how the suffixes would transform their words.

As they splashed around, each word changed in surprising ways. "Joy" became "joyful," spreading happiness all around. "Hope" turned into "hopeless," teaching them about the absence of hope. "Play" transformed into "playful," showing a fun and energetic nature. "Rain" became "rainy," describing the weather. "Wonder" turned into "wonderful," filling everyone with amazement.

The friends had fun creating new words and learning how suffixes could change the meanings of their favorite words. They left the Suffix Splash with a better understanding of how suffixes work and how they can use them in their own writing.

1. Joy ☐　　　　**2. Play** ☐　　　　**3. Wonder** ☐

_____　　　　_____　　　　_____

4. Hope ☐　　　　**5. Rain** ☐

_____　　　　_____

Suffixes
-ful　　-less　　-ing　　-ed　　-ly

Thumbs Up For A Job Well Done!

Activity 13   Unit 1   CCSS: RF.2.3

Consonant Cluster Crunch

Consonant Cluster Candy Shop

In the magical town of Wordland, there was a special candy shop known for its Consonant Cluster Crunch candies. Each candy wrapper was labeled with a consonant cluster like "sl," "fl," "br," and "th." Children loved discovering new words while enjoying these sweets.

One day, friends Liam, Emma, Sophia, and Noah visited the shop. Mr. Sweets, the shop owner, explained the game: each child had to find a candy with a consonant cluster and see what word was inside. Liam found "sl-" and discovered slide. Emma picked "fl-" and got float. Sophia chose "th-" and found throw. Noah selected "br-" and found bread. They even found a special candy with "gr-" and discovered grass inside.

Mr. Sweets encouraged them to match the candies with their consonant clusters and write the full word on an empty wrapper. If they had a favorite word, they could draw a candy bow on it. The friends had a fantastic time learning about consonant clusters and couldn't wait to visit the candy shop again.

Instructions

Read the story about the friends visiting the Consonant Cluster Candy Shop. Draw lines to match each candy (word) with its correct consonant cluster wrapper. Write the full word on the empty wrapper. If you have a favorite word, draw a bow on it.

Way To Go, Smart Cookie!

Activity 14 — Unit 1 — CCSS: RF.2.3d

Vowel Team Tag

Tagging Fun in Letterville Park

In the small town of Letterville, the children loved a special game called Vowel Team Tag. One sunny day, they gathered in the park to play. Mia had "meat" written on her tag and was looking for someone with "-**ea**-". Jack had the word "boat" and needed to find "-**oa**-". Lily with "seed" was searching for "-**ee**-", while Max with "train" and Zoe with "day" were looking for different vowel teams. They ran around the park, laughing and tagging each other, learning new words and sounds as they played.

Instructions

1. Look at the words on the left. These are the tags the kids are wearing.
2. Connect each word to its vowel team partner on the right.

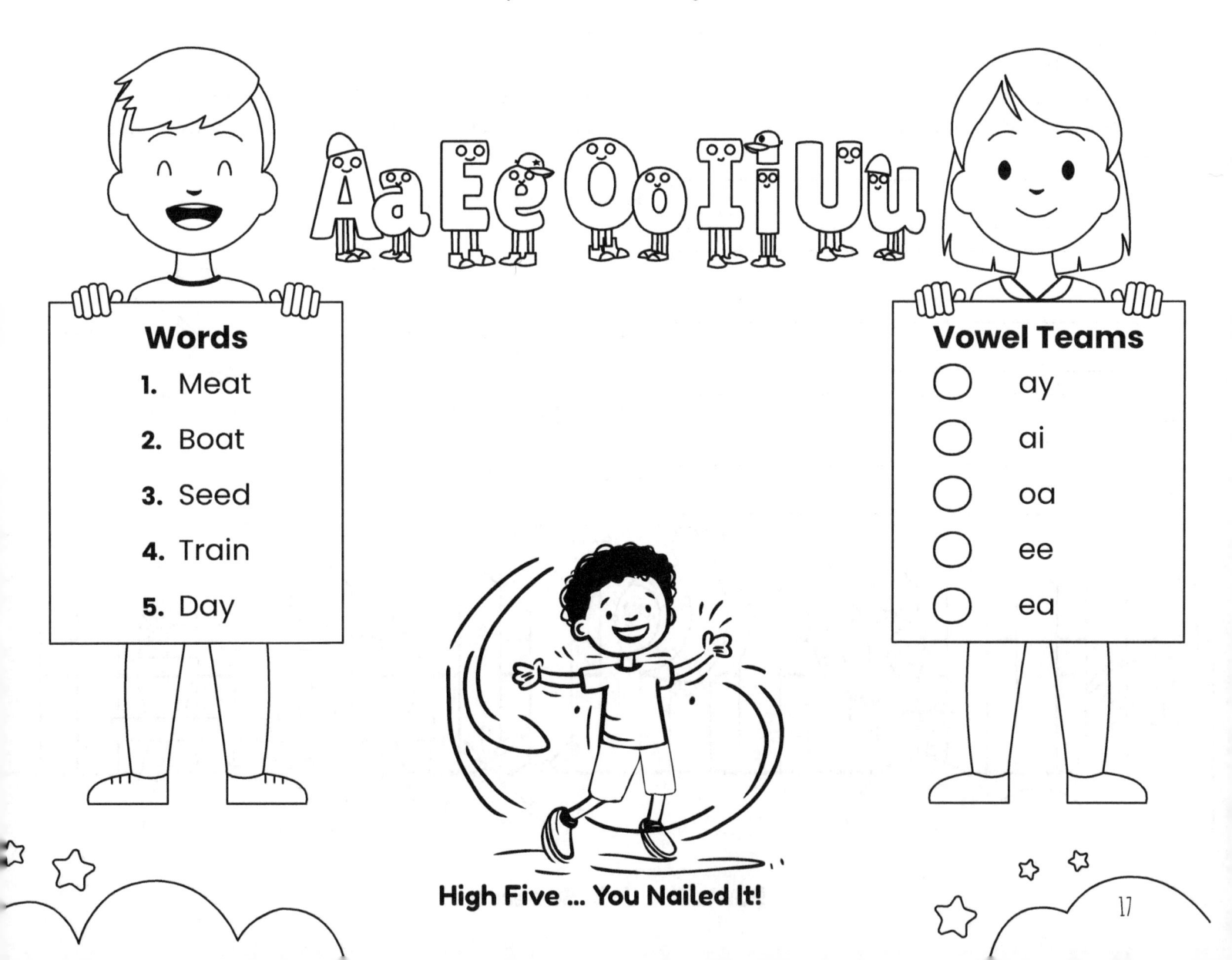

Words
1. Meat
2. Boat
3. Seed
4. Train
5. Day

Vowel Teams
- ay
- ai
- oa
- ee
- ea

High Five ... You Nailed It!

Activity 15 — **Unit 1** — CCSS: RF.2.3e

The Alphabetville Spelling Bee

The Spelling Bee

The annual Spelling Bee was the biggest event of the year. Emma, a second grader, was excited to compete after practicing for weeks. She was ready to spell words like 'cloud,' 'flower,' 'happy,' 'garden,' and 'butterfly.'

As Emma's turn approached, she took a deep breath to stay calm. The first word was cloud. She spelled it correctly, picturing the fluffy clouds in the sky. Next, she was asked to spell flower, which reminded her of the bright blooms in her garden. She spelled it with confidence.

The competition became more challenging, but Emma stayed focused. The word happy made her think of the joyful moments with her friends, so she spelled it easily. The final word was butterfly. Emma remembered the butterflies she watched in her backyard and spelled it perfectly.

Instructions

Imagine you are participating in the Alphabetville Spelling Bee with Emma. Think about the words from the story related to a garden. Now, try to spell each word on the lines below. No peeking back at the story!

1. _____ **Hint:** You see it in the sky.

2. _____ **Hint:** It's colorful and grows in the ground.

3. _____ **Hint:** The opposite of sad.

4. _____ **Hint:** A place with plants and flowers.

5. _____ **Hint:** A beautiful insect with wings.

Fantastic Job, Superstar!

Activity 16 — **Unit 1** — CCSS: RF.2.3

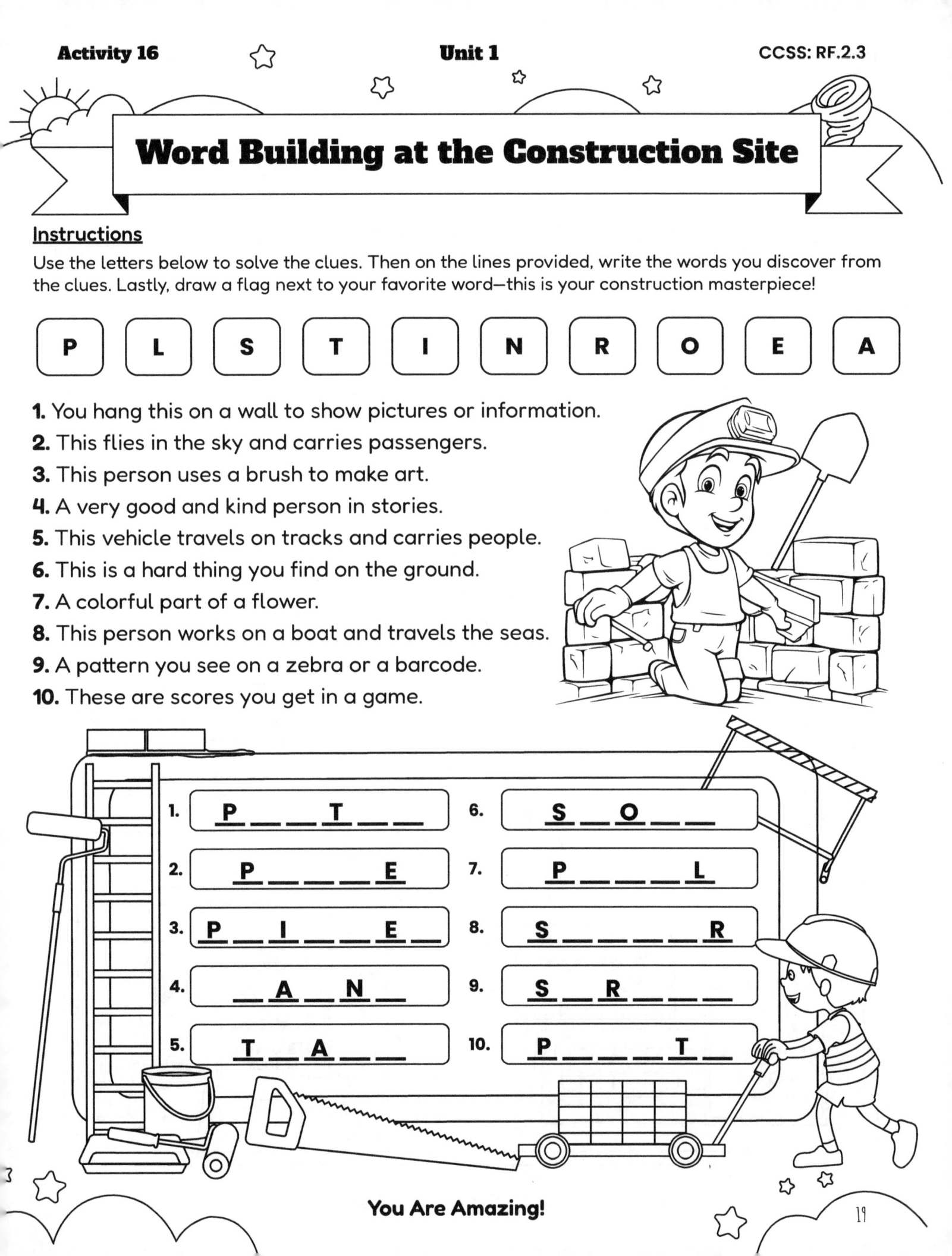

Word Building at the Construction Site

Instructions

Use the letters below to solve the clues. Then on the lines provided, write the words you discover from the clues. Lastly, draw a flag next to your favorite word—this is your construction masterpiece!

P L S T I N R O E A

1. You hang this on a wall to show pictures or information.
2. This flies in the sky and carries passengers.
3. This person uses a brush to make art.
4. A very good and kind person in stories.
5. This vehicle travels on tracks and carries people.
6. This is a hard thing you find on the ground.
7. A colorful part of a flower.
8. This person works on a boat and travels the seas.
9. A pattern you see on a zebra or a barcode.
10. These are scores you get in a game.

1. P _ T _ _
2. P _ _ _ E
3. P _ I _ E _
4. _ A N _
5. T _ A _ _
6. S _ O _
7. P _ _ _ L
8. S _ _ _ R
9. S _ R _ _ _
10. P _ _ _ T

You Are Amazing!

Activity 17   Unit 1   CCSS: RF.2.3e

The Puzzleton Library Mystery

Lucy's Library Riddles

Lucy skipped down the library aisles with a book of riddles. Each page had a fun challenge for her. There were blanks in the sentences where words should be, with mixed-up letters beside them as hints.

The first riddle said, "When the sky is gray, it gives us **(1)** _____." Lucy thought about it and then wrote down her answer.

Next, she read, "The **(2)** _____ in the sky makes the day bright." She figured out the jumble and filled in the blank.

She then read that a bee is an example of an **(3)** _____." Lucy knew this one and filled in the answer with a grin.

Another page showed, "To read tiny words, Mr. Lee puts on his **(4)** _____." Lucy guessed the right word and wrote it in.

The last riddle made Lucy smile. It said, "I love to read every **(5)** _____ about adventures and magic." She filled in the last blank proudly.

Instructions

Look at the scrambled words and think about what fits in each sentence. Fill in the blanks in Lucy's book with the words you find. After you've filled in the blanks, write each word you found on the lines below.

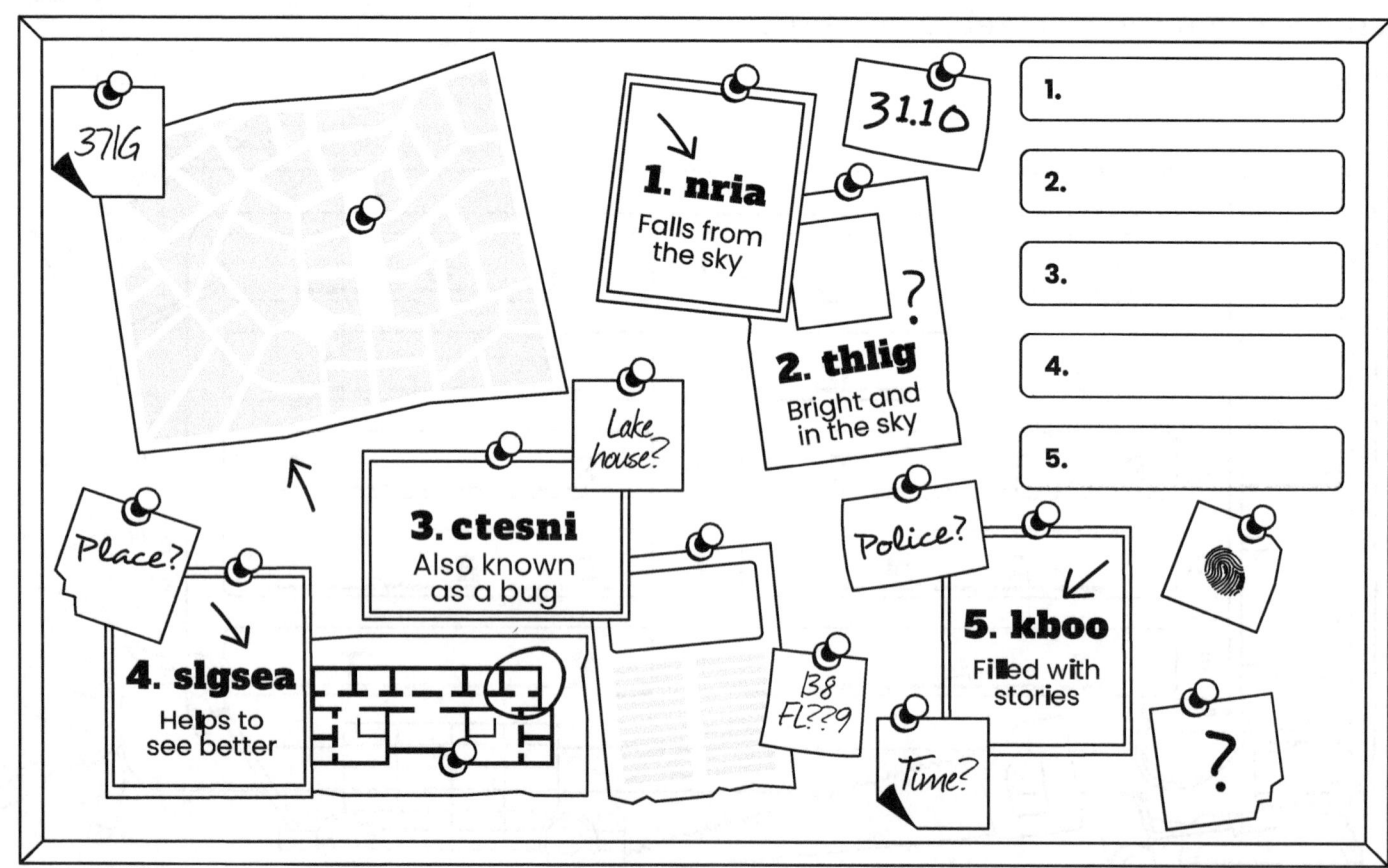

1. **nria** — Falls from the sky
2. **thlig** — Bright and in the sky
3. **ctesni** — Also known as a bug
4. **slgsea** — Helps to see better
5. **kboo** — Filled with stories

1. _____
2. _____
3. _____
4. _____
5. _____

Great Job, Detective!

Activity 18 **Unit 1** **CCSS: RF.2.3**

The Great Phonics Photo Hunt

Emma's Exciting Day

Emma had an exciting day planned. First, she would visit a farm to see the animals and maybe even feed them some cheese. Next, she was off to the harbor to watch the big ship coming into dock. After lunch, Emma planned to help her dad in the workshop, where he would teach her how to use a thumb tack and a wheel to make a toy car. And finally, if she finished all her chores, her mom promised to take her to see the ducks at the pond. Emma couldn't wait to throw bread crumbs to the duck and watch them quack and waddle.

Instructions

Read Emma's story and look for words that sound like 'ch,' 'sh,' 'th,' 'wh,' and 'ck.' Draw a line from each word to its matching sound. Then, draw a picture of each word in the box below it. Finally, color the star next to your favorite drawing.

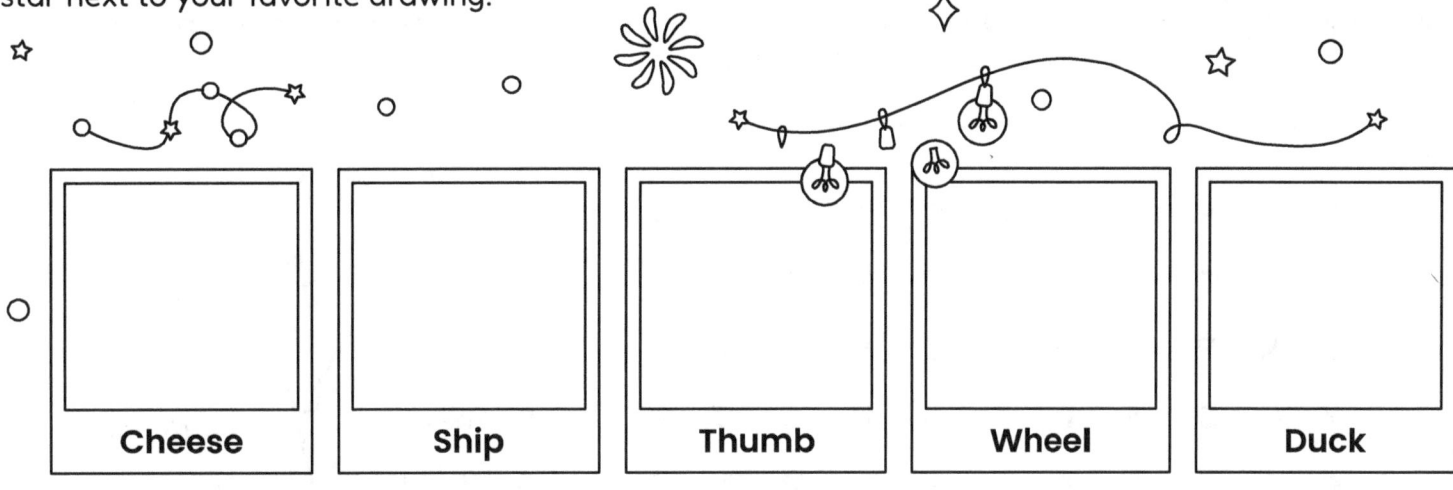

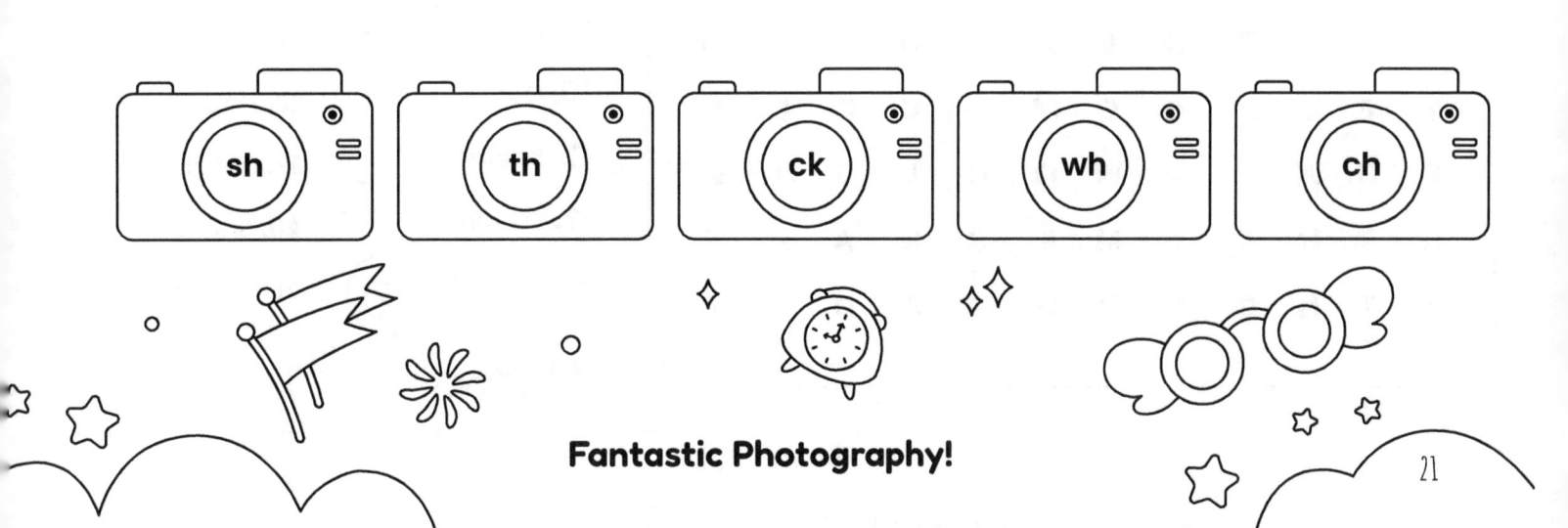

Cheese   **Ship**   **Thumb**   **Wheel**   **Duck**

sh   th   ck   wh   ch

Fantastic Photography!

Activity 19   **Unit 1**   CCSS: RF.2.3d

Panda Adventure Sight Word

Pandy's Hidden Treasure

In the green forests, a young panda named Pandy decided to explore beyond the familiar paths. They wandered past towering bamboo and saw the sunlight dancing on a hidden stream. Pandy wondered what treasures they might find there.

Then Pandy thought about how they could decorate the den with something special. Near the water's edge, Pandy picked up shiny stones. Each one had a unique sparkle that caught the light. Pandy knew they would make the perfect decoration.

These stones had been waiting for someone to share their beauty. Pandy was excited to show them to her family. They would all love the stones picked with love. With her paws full, Pandy headed back, eager to share the day's adventure.

They were happy to see Pandy return, and they all admired the stones picked from the stream. "We thought you were on an adventure," they said with smiles. And they were right; it had been quite a day for Pandy, full of discovery and wonder.

```
R O U Y Y D E C I D E D
S A B O U T F Q R Y D Y
H E X P L O R E N K S E
O Z Q D E R E D N A W R
W G I E N P A H W M M E
I P I C K E D N R Z B W
N E T O I Z R E H A D B
G S U R D E R E D N O W
Y E O A G Q M B U C D O
E H W T V W O U L D I W
H T H E N M K S H A R E
T T H G U O H T D D Q P
```

1. They
2. Were
3. Many
4. Then
5. These
6. Would
7. About
8. Your
9. Been
10. Out
11. Decided
12. Explore
13. Wandered
14. Saw
15. Wondered
16. Thought
17. Showing
18. Had
19. Decorat
20. Share
21. Picked

Great Job!

Activity 20 — **Unit 1** — CCSS: RF.2.3

The Word Wizard's Enchanted Quest

The Word Wizard

In the land of Alphabeta, the Word Wizard had a special quest. "To complete this quest," he announced to the children, "you must use your skills to fill in the magical blanks." The children gathered around, eager to begin.

"Our first puzzle," the wizard began, "is the opposite of 'lose.'" Lily thought hard and wrote her answer in the blank: "That's easy, it's _____!"
"Next up," the wizard continued, "we need something light as a feather." Max looked up and confidently filled in the next blank: "I know, it's a _____!"

Emma was already reaching for the third blank when the wizard asked for her favorite fruit. "I absolutely love _____!" she declared.
Oliver peered out the window as the sun began to set. "The opposite of night is _____," he mused, writing his answer.

Finally, Zoe gazed at the picture of the ocean on the wall. "I dream of sailing across the _____," she whispered, filling in the last blank.
The Word Wizard clapped with joy as each child successfully completed the quest.

Instructions

1. Use the clues to fill in the blanks in the Word Wizard's tale.
2. After you've filled in the blanks, check to see if they match the hints.
3. Next to the word you found the most challenging, draw a star!

1. ☐ **Hint:** Opposite of lose

2. ☐ **Hint:** Not heavy

3. ☐ **Hint:** A type of fruit

4. ☐ **Hint:** Opposite of night

5. ☐ **Hint:** A large body of water

Fantastic Reading!

Activity 21 **Unit 2** CCSS: RF.2.4, RL.2.10

Expressive Echoes

Mia the Magpie

Every morning, Mia the Magpie greeted the forest with her songs. All the animals loved to listen. One day, Sammy Squirrel shyly approached Mia. "Could I learn to sing too?" he asked. Mia smiled warmly. "Of course! Singing is for everyone!" Together, they practiced simple tunes. Soon, Sammy was singing with confidence.

As they sang, the other forest animals gathered around, enjoying the melody. "Your voice is wonderful," Mia encouraged Sammy, "and it's even better when you share it!" Sammy felt proud and happy.

He realized that with a little help, he could do anything.
"Let's sing together every morning," Mia suggested. Sammy nodded enthusiastically. "I'd love that!"

Instructions
Read Mia's story and notice the emotions and actions. Write or draw your favorite part in the box. Read it out loud with expression, using Mia's cheerful tone or Sammy's shy voice. Answer the discussion questions and think about what happens next.

Write and illustrate your favorite part here

Discussion Questions

1. Why do you think Sammy wanted to learn to sing?
_____
_____
_____
_____

2. How do you think singing makes Mia and Sammy feel?
_____
_____
_____
_____

Write a short continuation of Mia and Sammy's story or create a new story about another forest animal.

Fantastic Reading!

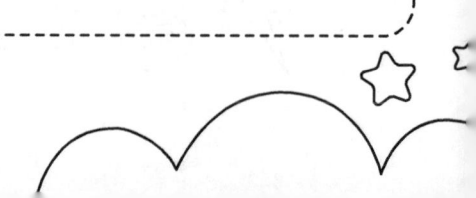

Activity 22 — **Unit 2** — CCSS: RF.2.3d, RF.2.4

Speedy Sight Words Challenge

Instructions
Pretend you're a race car driver at Sight Word Speedway! Set a one-minute timer and read as many words as you can before the timer ends. Keep track of how many words you read and try to beat your record next time. After the challenge, choose five challenging words and write a sentence with each.

List of Sight Words

Their	Write	People	There	First
Would	These	Before	Should	Been
About	Could	After	Another	Does
Which	Think	Every	Always	Were
Other	Because	Little	Around	Both
Come	Now	Out	Will	Too
Look	Some	Want	Up	Find
With	Very	Be	Down	Go

Number of words read in 1 minute: _____

Excellent! Choose five words you found challenging and write a entence with each.

1. _____
2. _____
3. _____
4. _____
5. _____

Great Job, Speed Reader!

Activity 23 — **Unit 2** — CCSS: RF.2.4, RL.2.6

Character Conversations in the Park

Instructions
Read each dialogue line, imagining you are the character speaking and thinking about how they feel. Try changing your voice to match the character's emotions. After reading, draw a picture of what you think Lila and Max look like based on their conversation.

A Sunny Day in the Park

Lila: "Look at that huge butterfly! I've never seen one like that before."
Max: "Wow! It's as big as my hand. Do you think it's looking for flowers?"
Lila: "Probably. I wish I could fly like that."
Max: "Me too! We'd soar above the trees and see the whole park."

Draw a scene from the conversation. What does the huge butterfly look like? How do Lila and Max express their wonder and excitement in your drawing?

What do you think happens next?

_____
_____
_____

Fantastic Job!

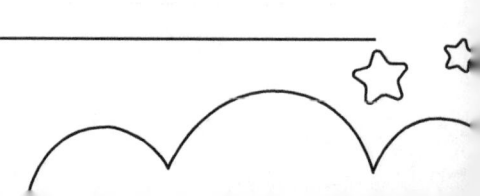

Activity 24 — **Unit 2** — CCSS: RF.2.4b, RL.2.4

The Rhythm of The Dancing Leaves

Instructions
Read the poem slowly and picture the scene in your mind. Then, read it again a bit faster, like leaves blowing in the wind. Think about how the poem feels different when you read it quickly.

The Dancing Leaves

Leaves on the trees, so still and high,
Suddenly twirl, and start to fly.
Dancing, swirling, all around,
Gently they touch the ground.

Golden, red, orange, and brown,
Nature's confetti all over the town.
They dance with joy, they dance with grace,
The leaves are in a happy race.

Write down how you felt reading the poem slowly vs. quickly

_____

_____

_____

Hooray For Being A Reading Superstar!

Activity 25　　　　**Unit 2**　　　　CCSS: RF.2.4a, RI.2.1

Discovering Sea Turtles

The Graceful Sea Turtles

Sea turtles are amazing animals that live in the ocean. They have been around for a very long time, even before your grandparents' grandparents were born! Sea turtles are different from turtles that live on land because they cannot hide their legs and head inside their shells. Their shells are special and help them swim fast.

Sea turtles love to swim in the ocean and eat things like plants and small sea animals. They can swim very far, from one place to another, to find food and to lay their eggs. When it's time to lay eggs, the mommy sea turtles go back to the beach where they were born. They lay their eggs in the sand and then go back to the ocean.

After some time, the eggs hatch, and baby turtles come out. These baby turtles hurry to the water to start their life in the ocean. This is how the life of a sea turtle begins.

1. What is different about sea turtles compared to land turtles?

_____

_____

2. What do sea turtles like to eat, and where do they live?

_____

_____

3. What do mommy sea turtles do when it's time to lay eggs?

_____

_____

_____

Did You Know?
Research one interesting fact about sea turtles and write it down.

28

Activity 26 — **Unit 2** — CCSS: RF.2.4, RL.2.4

Rhythm & Rhyme Relay

Instructions

1. Read each sentence out loud.
2. Circle the rhyming words in each sentence.
3. Now, read the sentences again faster and notice the rhythm.
4. Write your own rhyming sentence.

Rhythm & Rhyme Relay

1. The cat sat on a mat, wearing a fancy hat.
2. The frog on a log sang a song in the fog.
3. A mouse in the house found a tiny blouse.
4. The bear with brown hair sat in the chair.
5. A kite in the night shone so bright with light.
6. The duck in the truck had such good luck.
7. A goat in a boat wore a warm coat.
8. The bee by the tree was as busy as could be.

Write your own rhyming sentence below. Then share it with a friend or family member for extra fun.

You Are Amazing!

Activity 27 — **Unit 2** — CCSS: RF.2.4, SL.2.6

Emotion in Every Word

Instructions
1. Read each sentence and think about the feeling.
2. Use the color key to shade the heart next to each sentence with the color that matches the feeling.
3. Write why you feel that way in the space provided.

1. I just won the biggest teddy bear at the fair! ♡

   I feel this because ... _____
   _____

2. It's raining, and I left my homework outside. ♡

   I feel this because ... _____
   _____

3. The surprise party for my birthday was amazing! ♡

   I feel this because ... _____
   _____

4. I lost my favorite toy, and I can't find it anywhere. ♡

   I feel this because ... _____
   _____

5. The puppy licked my face, and I giggled uncontrollably. ♡

   I feel this because ... _____
   _____

Color Key

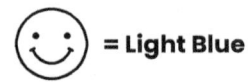

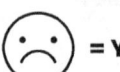

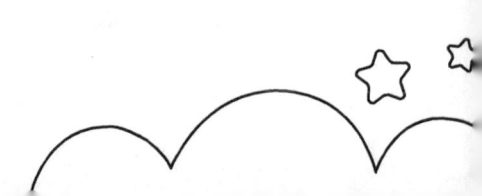

☺ = Light Blue   ☹ = Yellow   ☺ = Purple   😠 = Green   😆 = Red

Your Reading Is Truly Impressive

Activity 28 **Unit 2** CCSS: RF.2.3c, RF.2.4c

Multisyllabic Marathon

Instructions

1. Look at the word parts below.
2. Think about how they fit together.
3. Write the complete word next to it.

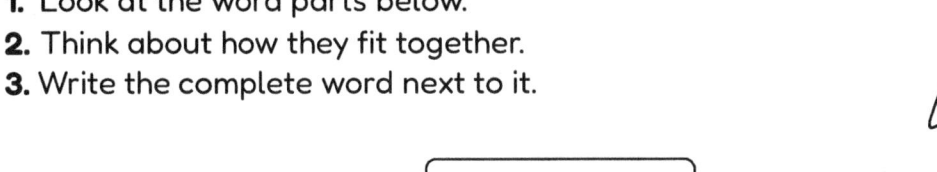

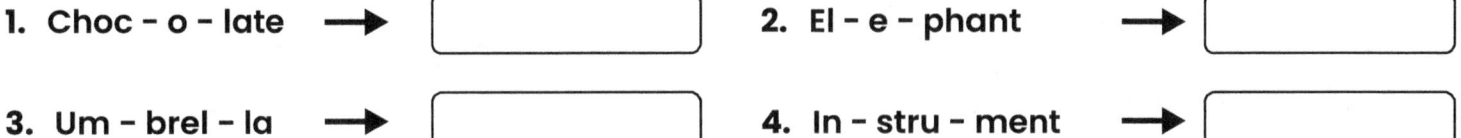

1. Choc - o - late → ☐

2. El - e - phant → ☐

3. Um - brel - la → ☐

4. In - stru - ment → ☐

5. But - ter - fly → ☐

After you've pieced together these big words, draw a picture of each one below. It's a great way to remember them and have fun!

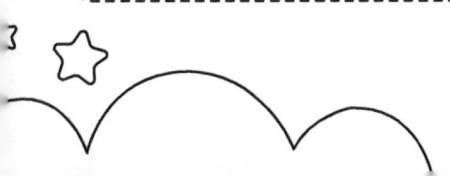

You Aced It—Congratulations!

Activity 29 **Unit 2** CCSS: RF.2.4, L.2.2

Punctuation Playhouse

Instructions

1. Read each sentence and bring the punctuation to life. Let your voice rise and fall with question marks and exclamation points, and pause briefly at commas.
2. Then write each sentence on the lines below, but change the punctuation. Notice how it changes the way you say it or what it means.

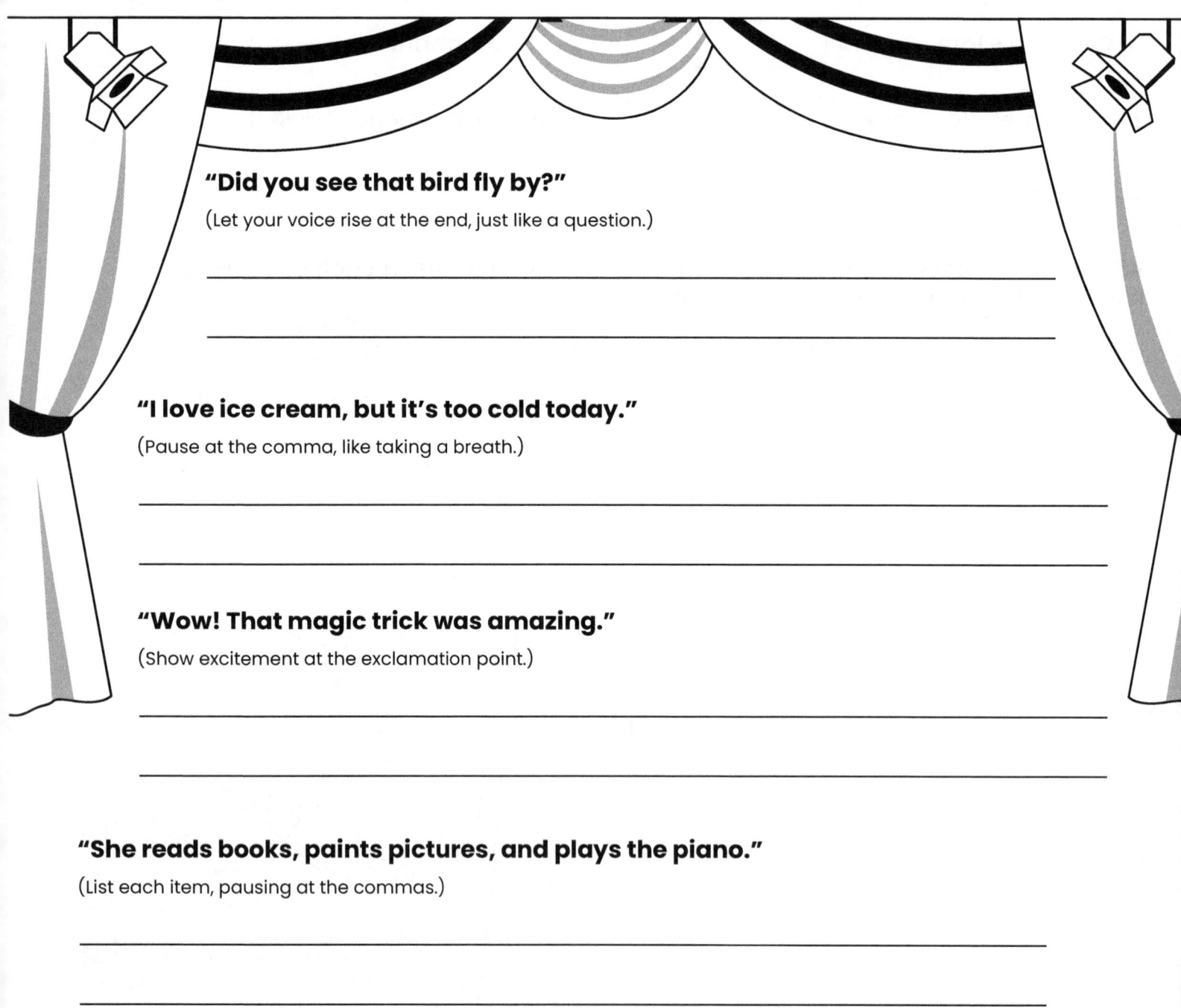

"Did you see that bird fly by?"
(Let your voice rise at the end, just like a question.)

_____

_____

"I love ice cream, but it's too cold today."
(Pause at the comma, like taking a breath.)

_____

_____

"Wow! That magic trick was amazing."
(Show excitement at the exclamation point.)

_____

_____

"She reads books, paints pictures, and plays the piano."
(List each item, pausing at the commas.)

_____

_____

What A Great Performance!

Activity 30 Unit 2 CCSS: RF.2.4, RL.2.4

Word Explorer Challenge

Instructions
1. Explore Words on the Map: As you find each word on the map, think about what it means.
2. Write the number of the definition next to the word on the map.
3. Use each word to make a new sentence and write it under the definition.

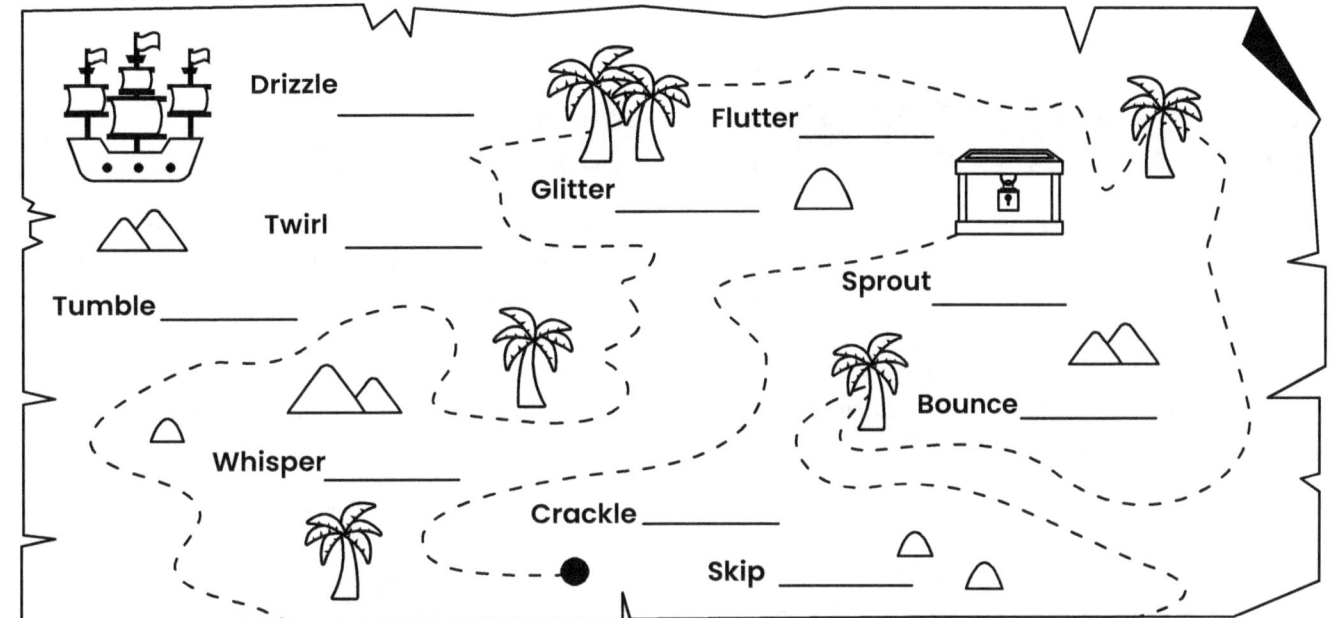

Words on the map:
- Drizzle _____
- Flutter _____
- Glitter _____
- Twirl _____
- Tumble _____
- Sprout _____
- Bounce _____
- Whisper _____
- Crackle _____
- Skip _____

1. To speak very softly.
_____
_____

2. To shine brightly with little flashes of light.
_____
_____

3. To move quickly back and forth, like wings.
_____
_____

4. To make short, sharp, snapping sounds.
_____
_____

5. To move with light, springy steps.
_____
_____

6. To spin around quickly.
_____
_____

7. To spring back after hitting something.
_____
_____

8. To begin to grow.
_____
_____

9. To rain lightly with small drops.
_____
_____

10. To fall or roll down suddenly.
_____
_____

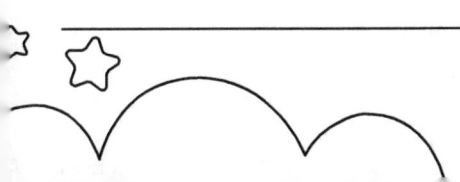

What A Successful Adventure!

Activity 31 — Unit 2 — CCSS: RF.2.4, SL.2.1

Campfire Storytime

Instructions

1. Sit with a friend as if you are around a campfire.
2. Take turns reading the stories. You read "The Moon's Lullaby," then your friend reads "The Playful Clouds."
3. Discuss what you liked about each story.
4. Then write about your favorite story and why you liked it.

Story 1: The Moon's Lullaby

Every night, Luna the moon sang a lullaby to the world. Her voice was soft and soothing, making the waves calm and the animals sleepy. One evening, a small owl named Oliver joined her. Together, they sang the most beautiful duet, filling the night with gentle melodies.

Story 2: The Playful Clouds

Up in the sky, two clouds named Clio and Cleon loved to play. They would shape-shift into animals, castles, and even umbrellas! One sunny day, they created a big heart in the sky, sending a message of love and joy to everyone below.

Think about which story you liked best and write why below.

_____

_____

_____

Fantastic Job!

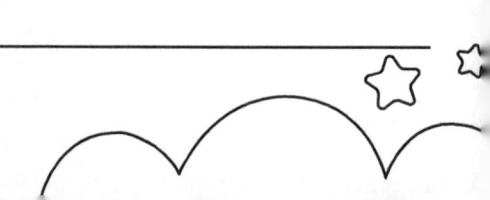

Activity 32 — **Unit 2** — CCSS: RF.2.4a, L.2.4a

Context Clues

Instructions

1. Become a word detective! Read the sentence with the bold word.
2. Use your detective skills to figure out what the word means based on the sentence.
3. Solve the mystery by answering the question about the word right below the sentence.

Craking Mysterious Words

1. The puppy was **energetic**, running around the yard all day.
What do you think **"energetic"** means?
_____

2. She felt **proud** when she completed her project.
How did the girl feel when she was **"proud"**?
_____

3. The treasure was hidden **beneath** the old oak tree.
Where was the treasure if it was **"beneath"**?
_____

4. His idea was **brilliant**, and everyone loved it.
If something is **"brilliant"**, is it good or bad?
_____

5. The cat was **curious** as it explored the new house.
If someone is **"curious"**, are they interested or bored?
_____

Your Turn!

Write a sentence of your own using one of the bold words above.

_____
_____

Excellent Detective Work!

Activity 33 Unit 2 CCSS: RF.2.4, RI.2.2

Silent Reading Reflection

The Marvelous World of Honeybees

Honeybees are small insects with a big job in nature. They fly around gardens and fields, visiting lots of flowers. They use their long tongues to drink a sweet liquid called nectar. They take this nectar back to their homes, called hives, and make it into yummy honey.

Honeybees also help flowers and plants. When they visit flowers, tiny bits of pollen stick to their bodies. They carry this pollen to other flowers, which helps the plants make fruits and seeds. Many fruits and vegetables we eat need bees to grow.

In their hive, honeybees live together and work as a team. The queen bee lays eggs. Worker bees take care of the hive and find nectar. Drone bees have a special job in helping make new bees. All the bees work together to keep their hive strong and to help plants outside.

TRUE	FALSE	1. Pollen sticks to honeybees' bodies as they move between flowers
TRUE	FALSE	2. Honeybees use their wings to collect nectar from flowers.
TRUE	FALSE	3. Honeybees turn nectar into honey in their hives.
TRUE	FALSE	4. Only the queen bee in the hive collects nectar.
TRUE	FALSE	5. Honeybees help plants produce fruits and seeds.

Write a short summary of the story

_____
_____
_____
_____

Wow! You're Incredible!

Activity 34   **Unit 2**   CCSS: RF.2.4, SL.2.2

Melody of Words

Instructions

1. Look at each sentence and notice the musical notes.
2. Let your voice follow the musical notes as you read each sentence aloud.
3. Enjoy the melody of the words!

Musical Tones

- ♫ I love to ♫ play outside ♫ especially ♫ in the park ♫.
- ♫ The cat ♫ sat on the ♫ windowsil ♫, watching ♫ the world ♫.
- ♫ Every morning ♫, I eat ♫ cereal ♫ and drink ♫ orange juice ♫.
- ♫ On weekends ♫, we go to the ♫ movies ♫ or the ♫ zoo ♫.
- ♫ My best friend ♫ is funny and ♫ always makes me laugh ♫.

Try creating your own sentence with musical notes. Write it down then read it aloud.

_____
_____
_____
_____

You're A Reading Musician!

Activity 35 **Unit 2** CCSS: RF.2.3, RF.2.4

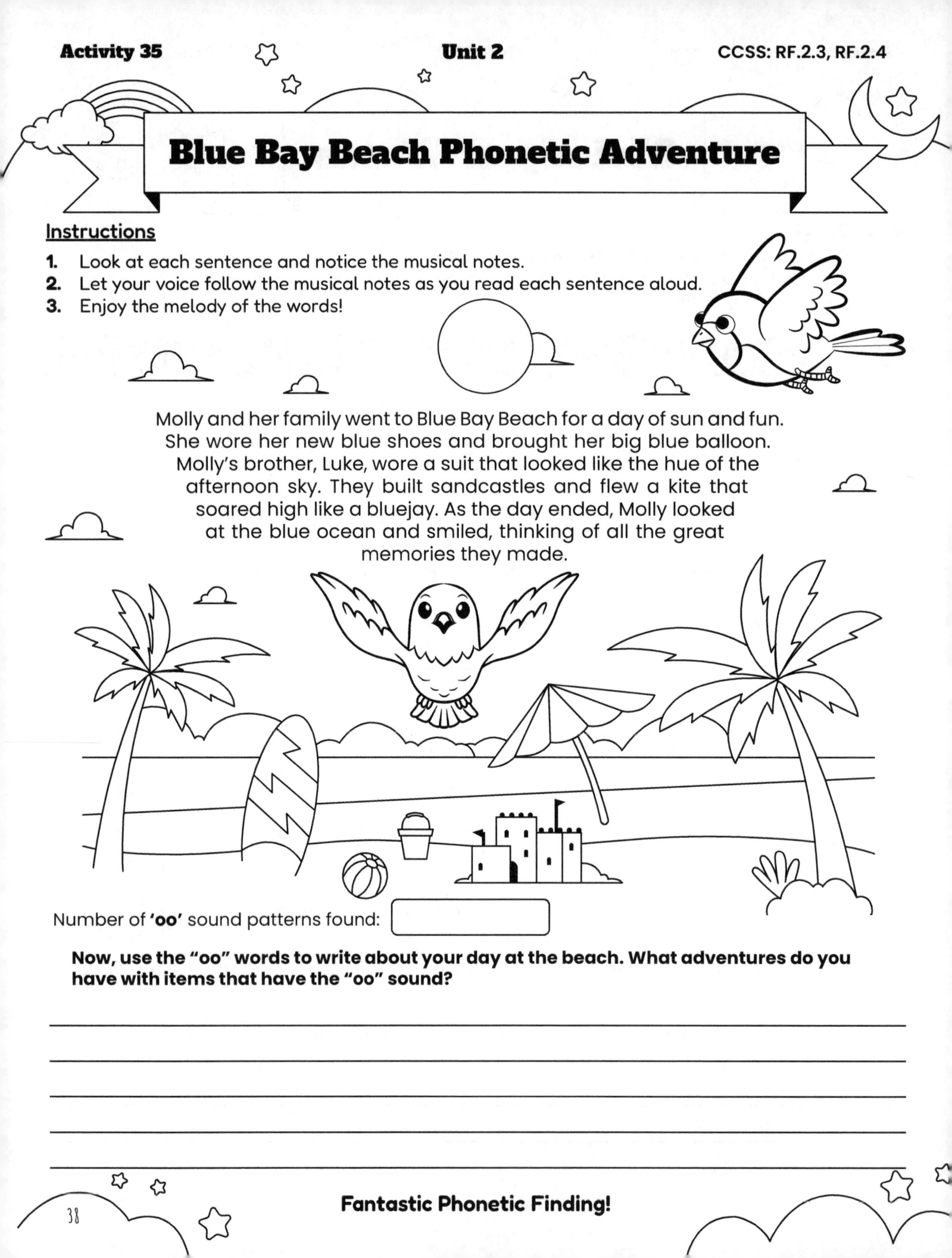

Blue Bay Beach Phonetic Adventure

Instructions
1. Look at each sentence and notice the musical notes.
2. Let your voice follow the musical notes as you read each sentence aloud.
3. Enjoy the melody of the words!

Molly and her family went to Blue Bay Beach for a day of sun and fun. She wore her new blue shoes and brought her big blue balloon. Molly's brother, Luke, wore a suit that looked like the hue of the afternoon sky. They built sandcastles and flew a kite that soared high like a bluejay. As the day ended, Molly looked at the blue ocean and smiled, thinking of all the great memories they made.

Number of 'oo' sound patterns found: _____

Now, use the "oo" words to write about your day at the beach. What adventures do you have with items that have the "oo" sound?

_____
_____
_____
_____
_____

Fantastic Phonetic Finding!

Activity 36 — **Unit 2** — CCSS: RF.2.4, RF.2.3d

Word Race Challenge

Instructions
Get set for a thrilling word race! Below is a list of exciting words. Set a timer for one minute and read as many words as you can, clearly and correctly. Keep track of your score and try to beat it next time.

Ready, Set, Read!

1. Puppy
2. Rainbow
3. Cupcake
4. Dolphin
5. Balloon
6. Castle
7. Pirate
8. Garden
9. Bicycle
10. Dragon
11. Picnic
12. Snowflake
13. Kangaroo
14. Marshmallow
15. Strawberry
16. Rocket
17. Treasure
18. Butterfly
19. Elephant
20. Chocolate
21. Monster
22. Diamond
23. Squirrel
24. Volcano
25. Whistle
26. Jungle
27. Penguin
28. Skeleton

Number of words read in 1 minute: _____

Choose your favorite word from the list and create a fun, silly sentence with it.

_____
_____
_____

You're A Reading Musician!

Activity 37 — Unit 2 — CCSS: RF.2.4, L.2.2

Imaginary Punctuation Play

Instructions
Read the sentences out loud and use the punctuation marks to help you. Write how they make you read differently. Then, make up your own sentence with a punctuation mark!

A Sunny Day in the Park

"The sun is shining, and the birds are singing."
(Pause at the comma, like taking a breath.)
_____
_____

"Wow! That was an incredible magic trick."
(Show excitement at the exclamation point.)
_____
_____

"Can you help me find my lost toy?"
(Let your voice rise at the question mark.)
_____
_____

"I love ice cream; chocolate is my favorite flavor."
(Pause at the semicolon, showing a connection between two ideas.)
_____
_____

"Let's go to the park, play on the swings, and have a picnic."
(Pause at each comma, as if listing each activity.)
_____
_____

Write a sentence using an exclamation point. Read it aloud and describe how it feels.
_____
_____

You're A Punctuation Superstar!

Activity 38 Unit 2 CCSS: RF.2.3, RF.2.4

Digraph Drama Theater

Instructions

Read each sentence below and act it out, emphasizing the sounds of the digraphs (like 'sh' in 'ship' or 'ph' in 'phone'). Let your voice and actions make the sounds stand out as you perform. After acting, write your own sentence using a digraph and try performing it too!

1. "The **sh**ip sailed smoothly on the **sh**ining sea."
   (Make the "sh" sound with a gesture like sailing a ship.)

2. "She **sh**ared her **sh**oes with her little sister."
   (Act out sharing shoes with a big smile.)

3. "The **gh**ost was **wh**ispering in the haunted house."
   (Use a spooky voice for "gh" and "wh.")

4. "The fish **sp**lashed and **thr**ashed in the shallow water."
   (Pretend a fish splashing in water.)

5. "The **ph**one rang loudly, making everyone jump."
   (Pretend to be startled by a loud phone ring.)

What did you enjoy most about acting out the digraphs?

_____

_____

_____

What A Brilliant Performance, Bravo!

Activity 39   Unit 2   CCSS: RF.2.3c, RF.2.4

Syllable Sorting Race

Instructions

Sort the words below into the correct bins based on whether they have 1, 2, or 3 syllables, then read each word aloud. Once you've sorted and read the words, use one word from each bin to create a silly sentence.

Words to Sort

- Adventure
- Elephant
- Park
- Chocolate
- Day
- Butterfly
- Universe
- Celebrate
- Sunflower

1 Syllable   **2 Syllables**   **3 Syllable**

After sorting the words, write 3 silly sentences using any word from each syllable bin.

1) _____

2) _____

3) _____

Amazing Sorting & Reading!

Activity 40 Unit 2 CCSS: RF.2.4, SL.2.6

Emotion Expression Theater

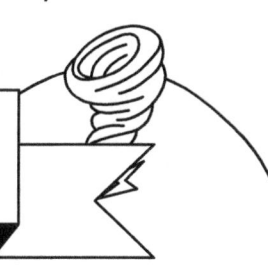

Instructions

Read each sentence out loud using the given emotion. Then in the next section, match each sentence to the best emotion from the word bank. Think about how different emotions can change what the sentence means.

Emotion Word Bank

| Surprised | Excited | Sad | Anxious | Grateful |

Expressive Reading

1. Wow! The cat climbed the tree. — Surprised
2. I forgot my lunch at home. — Sad
3. Hooray! We're having a pizza party! — Excited
4. He kindly shared his toys with me. — Grateful
5. Oh no! The movie starts in ten minutes. — Anxious

Matching Emotions

1. The cat climbed the tree.

2. I forgot my lunch at home.

3. We're having a pizza party?

4. He shared his toys with me.

5. The movie starts in ten minutes.

Brilliant Performance!

Activity 41 — **Unit 3** — CCSS: RI.2.2, RI.2.8

Main Idea Detective Agency

Instructions
For each interesting paragraph, match it with the main idea listed at the top. Write the correct main idea below its paragraph. After you match them, draw a star next to your favorite one.

Main Ideas
1. Trees are helpful for nature and animals.
2. Bees are busy insects that make honey.
3. The sun is important for our day and warmth.
4. Rain is important for plants and animals.

Interesting Paragraphs

A Bees are busy little insects. They fly from flower to flower to gather nectar, which they turn into honey back at their hive. They help flowers grow by spreading pollen.

Main Idea: _____

B The sun shines bright every day, making it light outside. It helps keep the Earth warm, which is important for plants to grow and for us to stay warm.

Main Idea: _____

C Trees are very important. They give us shade on sunny days and a place for birds to build nests. Trees also help make the air we breathe cleaner.

Main Idea: _____

D Rain is very important for the Earth. It helps plants grow by giving them water. It also fills rivers and lakes that animals use to drink and live in.

Main Idea: _____

Create your own interesting paragraph!
_____
_____

Main Idea:
_____
_____

What A Brilliant Performance, Bravo!

Activity 42 — **Unit 3** — CCSS: RL.2.3, RL.2.6

Character Emotion Theater

Instructions
Read each dialogue aloud and act out the emotion you think the character is feeling. Use the Emotion Word Bank to guess what the character might be feeling or thinking and write the emotion in the box next to each dialogue. After that, draw a picture that matches the dialogue and the emotion.

Emotion Word Bank
Worried   Excited   Comforted   Amazed   Proud   Grateful

Draw a picture

A. "I can't find my favorite toy! I just had it yesterday." – Mia

Emotion: _____

B. "Thanks for helping me with my homework, you're the best!" – Jake

Emotion: _____

C. "I practiced every day, and now I can play the song without any mistakes!" – Liam

Emotion: _____

D. "Look at the butterfly! It's so pretty and colorful." – Emma

Emotion: _____

E. "I'm a little scared of the dark, but I have my nightlight." – Sam

Emotion: _____

F. "Yay, we're going to the zoo tomorrow! I can't wait to see the elephants." – Olivia

Emotion: _____

Bravo!

Activity 43 Unit 3 CCSS: RI.2.3, RI.2.8

Fact or Opinion?

Instructions

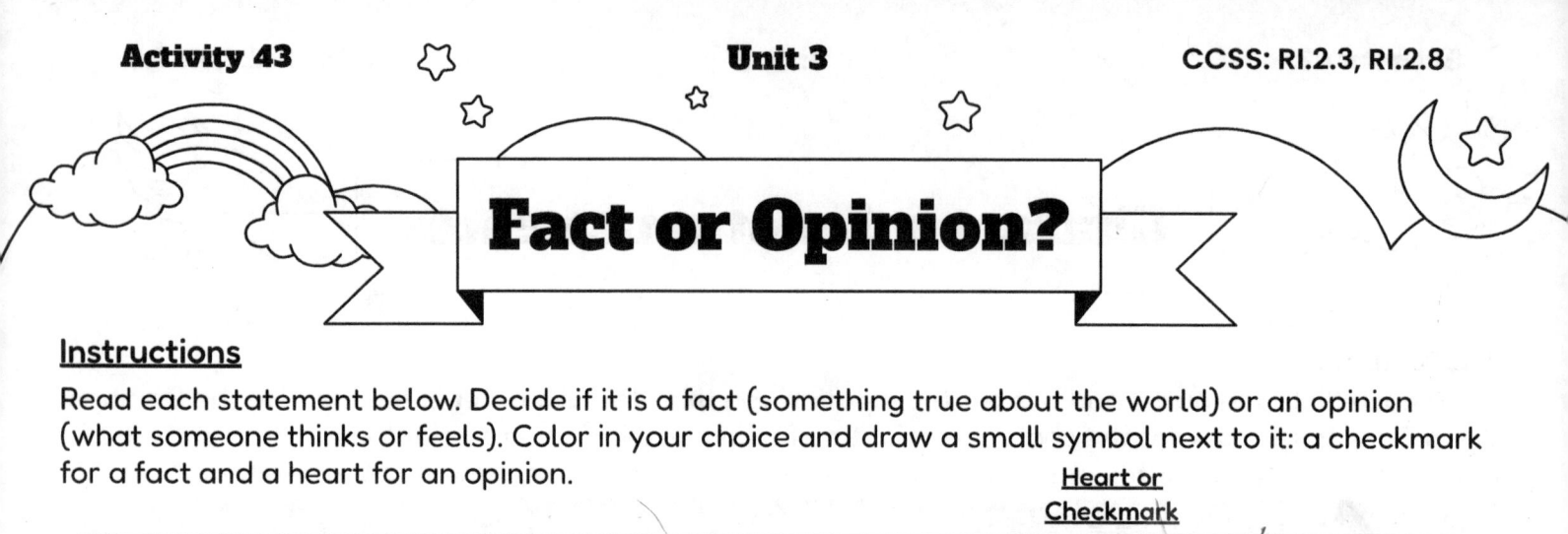

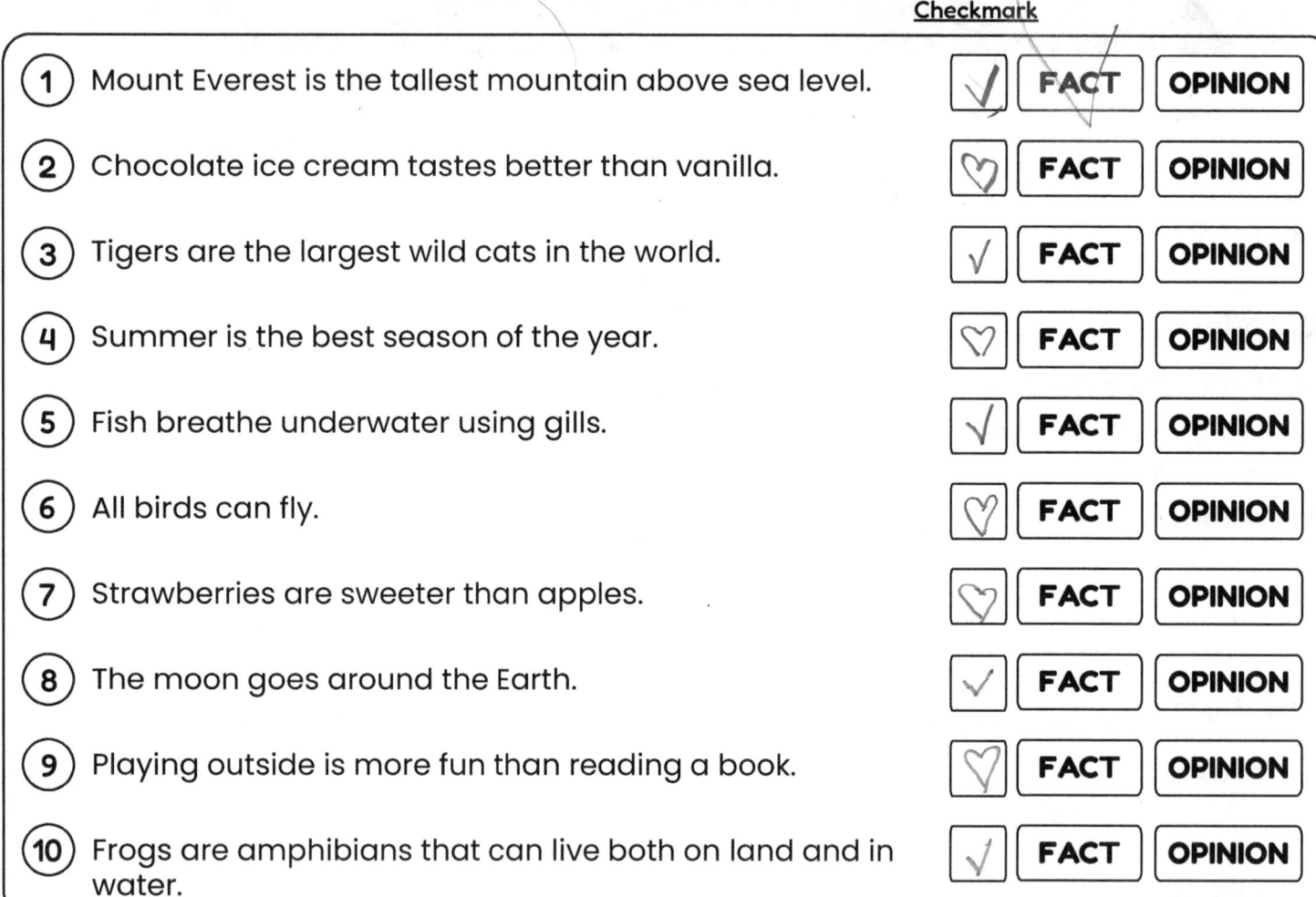

Read each statement below. Decide if it is a fact (something true about the world) or an opinion (what someone thinks or feels). Color in your choice and draw a small symbol next to it: a checkmark for a fact and a heart for an opinion.

Heart or Checkmark

1. Mount Everest is the tallest mountain above sea level. ✓ FACT | OPINION
2. Chocolate ice cream tastes better than vanilla. ♡ FACT | OPINION
3. Tigers are the largest wild cats in the world. ✓ FACT | OPINION
4. Summer is the best season of the year. ♡ FACT | OPINION
5. Fish breathe underwater using gills. ✓ FACT | OPINION
6. All birds can fly. ♡ FACT | OPINION
7. Strawberries are sweeter than apples. ♡ FACT | OPINION
8. The moon goes around the Earth. ✓ FACT | OPINION
9. Playing outside is more fun than reading a book. ♡ FACT | OPINION
10. Frogs are amphibians that can live both on land and in water. ✓ FACT | OPINION

Great Detective Work!

Activity 44 — **Unit 3** — CCSS: RL.2.1, RL.2.7

Setting the Scene

Instructions

Get ready to be an artist! Below are descriptions of different places. After reading each one, draw the scene as you picture it. What colors and shapes do you see in your mind?

The Garden

The garden was full of colors. There were red roses and pink tulips. A little pond was there with fish swimming under green leaves. Butterflies flew around, and there was a path by a big apple tree with red apples.

The Beach

The beach was quiet and pretty. The sand was soft and white. The water came up to the sand softly. Seagulls flew in the sky. There were umbrellas of many colors, and kids were making sandcastles.

The Forest

The forest had big trees that went up high. Light came through the leaves and made shapes on the ground. Squirrels ran up the trees. There was a stream with water going over rocks.

After drawing, think about what you would hear or smell in each place and write a sentence about each one.

The Garden _____

The Beach _____

The Forest _____

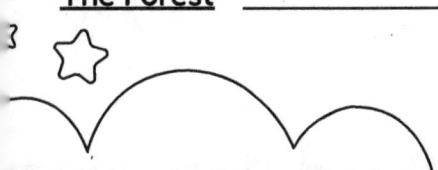

Great Job, Young Artist!

Activity 45 — **Unit 3** — CCSS: RL.2.5, RL.2.2

Story Time Sequencer

Instructions

Oh no, the steps to make a s'more got all mixed up! Read each step carefully, then correctly put the letters in order from the beginning to the end. Let's see if you can make the steps make sense again!

Sarah's S'more Adventure

A. Then, she put some marshmallows on top of the chocolate. — 1 ☐

B. First, Sarah decided to make a s'more. — 2 ☐

C. Finally, she took a bite and smiled, enjoying her tasty treat. — 3 ☐

D. After that, she placed a piece of chocolate on a graham cracker. — 4 ☐

E. Sarah found all the ingredients in the kitchen. — 5 ☐

F. She carefully roasted the marshmallows over the stove. — 6 ☐

G. Sarah put another graham cracker on top to complete her s'more. — 7 ☐

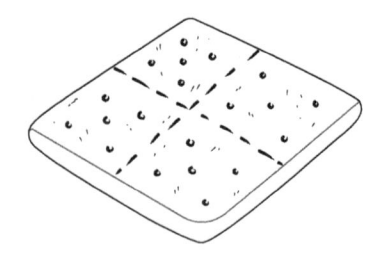

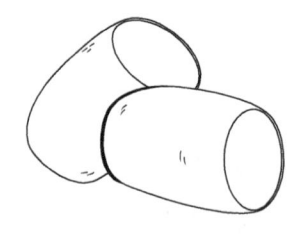

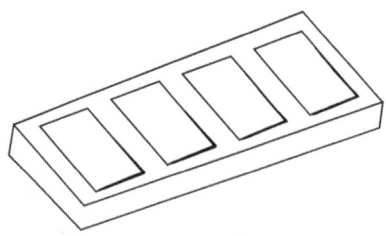

Draw a picture of your favorite part of making s'mores.

Great Job, Story Organizer!

Activity 46 — Unit 3 — CCSS: RI.2.4, L.2.4

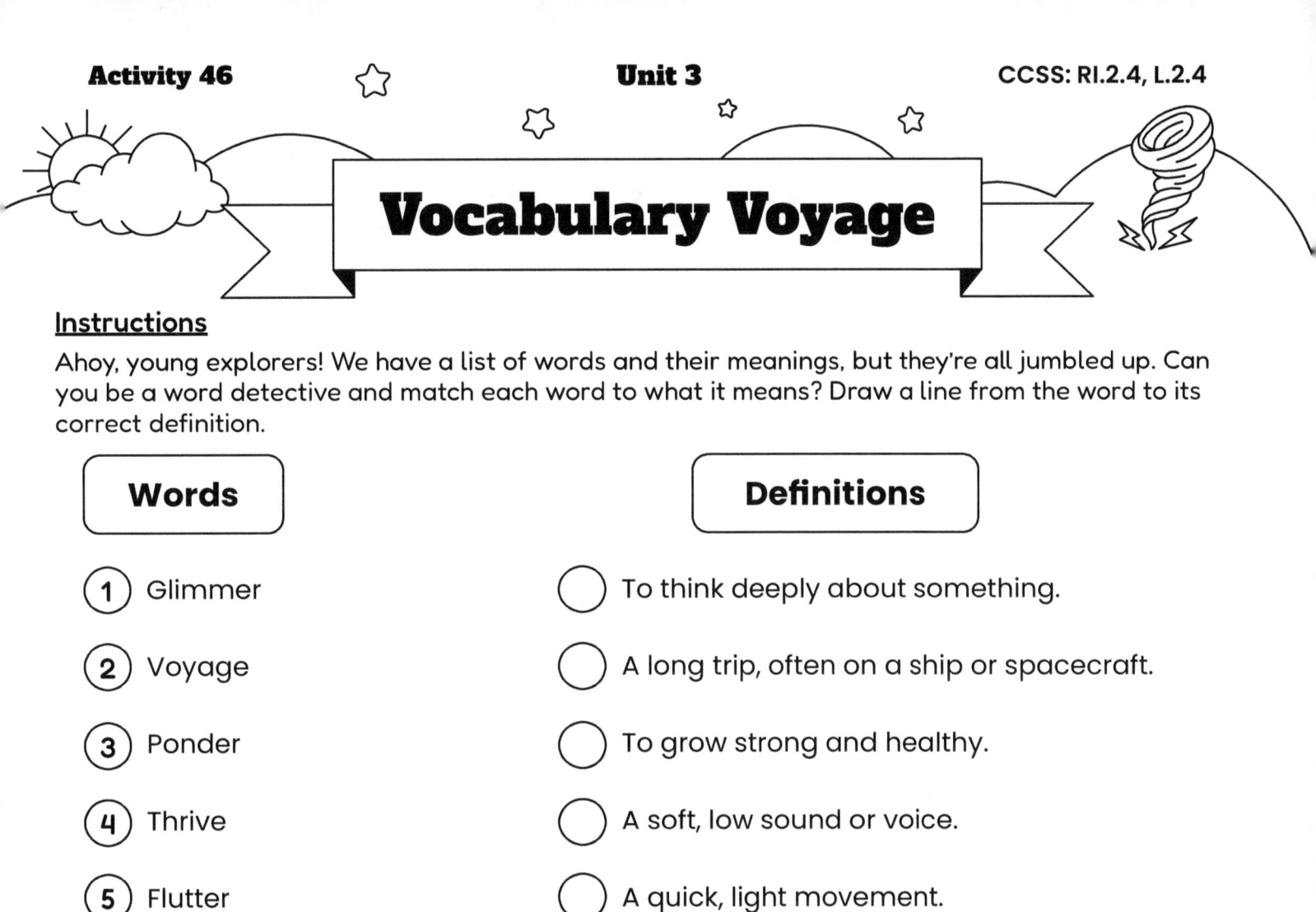

Vocabulary Voyage

Instructions

Ahoy, young explorers! We have a list of words and their meanings, but they're all jumbled up. Can you be a word detective and match each word to what it means? Draw a line from the word to its correct definition.

Words

1. Glimmer
2. Voyage
3. Ponder
4. Thrive
5. Flutter
6. Whisper

Definitions

- To think deeply about something.
- A long trip, often on a ship or spacecraft.
- To grow strong and healthy.
- A soft, low sound or voice.
- A quick, light movement.
- A soft, gentle light that seems to shake a little.

Choose a word from above and write a sentence using it. Then draw a small picture about your sentence that shows what your word means.

Awesome Job!

Activity 47 — **Unit 3** — CCSS: RL.2.1, RL.2.5

Story Solution Sleuth

Instructions

Some stories have tricky problems, and they need your help to find the right solutions. Put on your detective hat and help solve the story problems! Match each problem to its solution by writing the problem number next to the correct solution letter.

Problems

1. Jenny wanted to bake a cake for her mom's birthday, but she didn't have any eggs.

2. Max's kite got stuck in a tree, and he couldn't reach it.

3. Lisa wanted to read a book at night, but her room was too dark.

4. Sam lost his favorite toy car and couldn't find it anywhere.

5. Emma's plant was wilting because she forgot to water it.

Solutions

A. _____ He cleaned his room and found his toy car under the bed.

B. _____ She gave her plant some water, and it started to look healthy again.

C. _____ He used a long stick to carefully get his kite down from the tree.

D. _____ She borrowed a flashlight from her brother and continued reading.

E. _____ She went to her neighbor's house and kindly asked for some eggs.

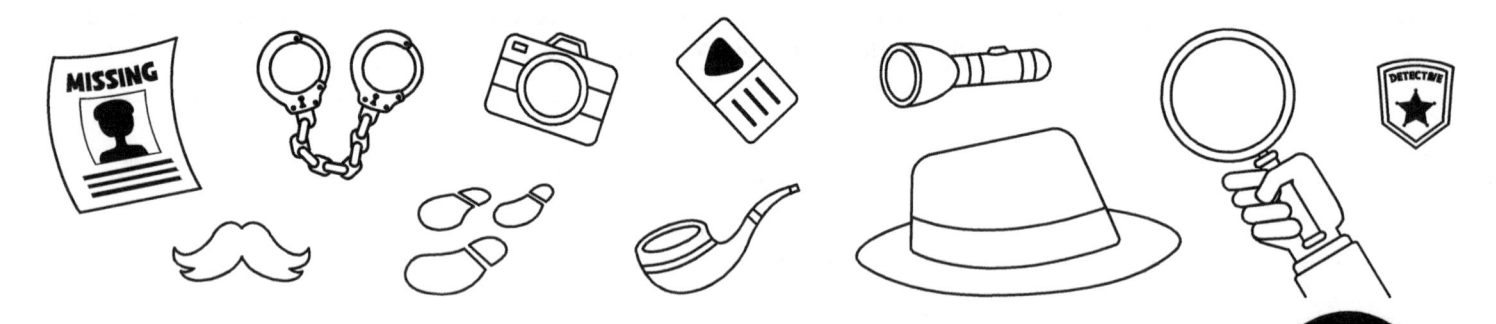

Think of a problem you've had and how you solved it. Write a short story about it.

_____

_____

You're Born To Be A Problem' Solver!

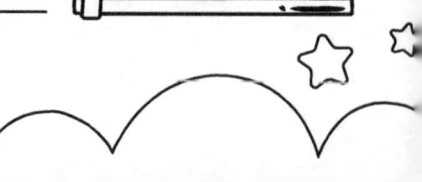

Activity 48 | **Unit 3** | CCSS: RI.2.3, RL.2.3

Cause and Effect Connect

Instructions

1. Read the story below to see how different events lead to specific outcomes.
2. Match each cause with its correct effect from the story.

A Rainy Day Adventure

One rainy morning, Tim was feeling nervous about his math test. He had studied hard the night before, hoping to do well. His sister Jenny, however, was running late and skipped breakfast. Their mom, Sara, went outside to water the plants, even though it was already raining. As they left the house, the wind blew strongly, causing leaves and small branches to scatter everywhere.

After school, Tim came home with an excellent score on his test. Jenny, on the other hand, felt very hungry by lunchtime because she had skipped breakfast. Sara noticed that the flowers in her garden were blooming beautifully, thanks to the extra water. Tim and Jenny had fun jumping in the puddles that had formed on the streets and sidewalks from the morning rain.

Cause

1. It rained heavily all day.
2. Tim studied hard for his math test.
3. Jenny skipped breakfast in the morning.
4. The wind blew strongly during the night.
5. Sara watered her plants every day.

Effect

A. Jenny felt very hungry by lunchtime.
B. Puddles formed on the streets and sidewalks.
C. Tim got an excellent score on his test.
D. The flowers in Sara's garden bloomed beautifully.
E. Leaves and small branches were scattered in the yard.

Think of a cause and effect from your own life and write a short sentence about it.

Cause: _____

Effect: _____

You're A Cause And Effect Expert!

Activity 49 — Unit 3 — CCSS: RL.2.2, RL.2.6

The Big Ideas

Instructions

Read the short stories below and think about the big idea or lesson in each one. Then, write down what you think the main idea of each story is. Remember, the main idea is the important lesson the story is teaching us.

Mia's Art Adventure

Mia always loved to draw, but she was afraid to show her art because she thought others might not like it. One day, her teacher saw her drawing and said she should put it in the school art show. Mia was nervous but said yes. Many people liked her art, and she even won a prize. Mia learned to believe in herself.

Sam's New Friend

Sam was new in school and felt alone. He saw a boy named Alex playing alone during recess and decided to ask if he could play too. Alex smiled and said yes. They played and laughed together. Sam learned that making friends starts with saying hello.

Lily & the Lost Puppy

Lily found a lost puppy in the park. She was worried and knew she had to help. She made posters and put them all around her neighborhood. The next day, a family saw the poster and called Lily. They were so happy to find their lost puppy. Lily learned that helping others feels good.

Mia's Story _____
_____

Sam's Story _____
_____

Lily's Story _____
_____

Draw a small picture that represents the theme of each story.

You Make Learning Look Easy—Amazing!

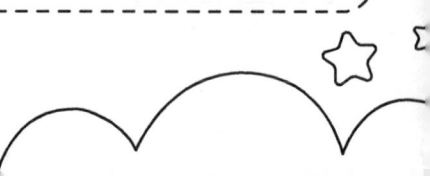

Activity 50 Unit 3 CCSS: RI.2.1, RI.2.6

Penguin Facts Detective

Instructions
Let's become a penguin facts detective! Read the information about penguins below. Then, answer the questions to show what you learned.

Penguins are unique birds that can't fly and mostly live in chilly places in the Southern Hemisphere, especially in Antarctica.
Their black and white feathers help them blend in with the snowy land and the dark ocean.
Penguins love eating fish and tiny shrimp-like creatures called krill.

They move on ice by sliding on their bellies, which is called tobogganing. Penguins are great swimmers, using their wings like flippers. They take turns caring for their eggs, keeping them warm on their feet under a layer of feathers. This teamwork is vital for their chicks' survival.

1. Why can't penguins be seen easily by other animals in the water?
   _____

2. What are two things penguins like to eat?
   _____

3. How do penguins move quickly on ice?
   _____

4. What special way do penguins use their wings in the water?
   _____

5. How do penguin parents care for their eggs?
   _____

Wonderful Work!

Activity 51   Unit 3   CCSS: RL.2.4, RL.2.6

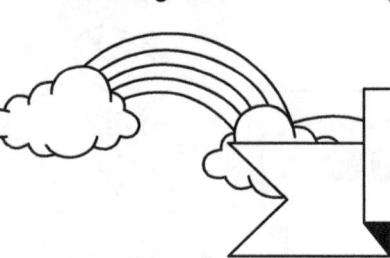

Poetic Discoveries

Instructions
Read the two fun poems below and imagine the scenes they describe. Think about what the poems are saying and how they make you feel. Then, answer the fun questions to discover more about each poem.

Poem 1: The Playful Wind

The wind plays tag, rushing by,
Whispering secrets, low and high.
It tickles the leaves, and bends the trees,
And brings the scent of flowers with ease.

Poem 2: The Smiling Sun

The sun smiles down on fields and towns,
Turning skies blue, chasing away frowns.
It warms the earth, lights up the day,
Makes flowers bloom and children play.

1. What games does the wind seem to play?

_____

2. What does the wind do to the leaves and trees?

_____

3. How do you think the wind makes the world around it feel?

_____

1. What does the sun do to the sky and the earth?

_____

2. How does the sun affect flowers and children?

_____

3. What feelings do you think the sun brings to the day?

_____

Fantastic Job!

Activity 52 **Unit 3** CCSS: RI.2.7, RI.2.3

Fruit Festival Graph Adventure

Instructions

We asked second graders about their favorite fruits for our festival. Look at the graph showing their choices and answer the questions. Can you figure out which fruit is the most popular of the festival?

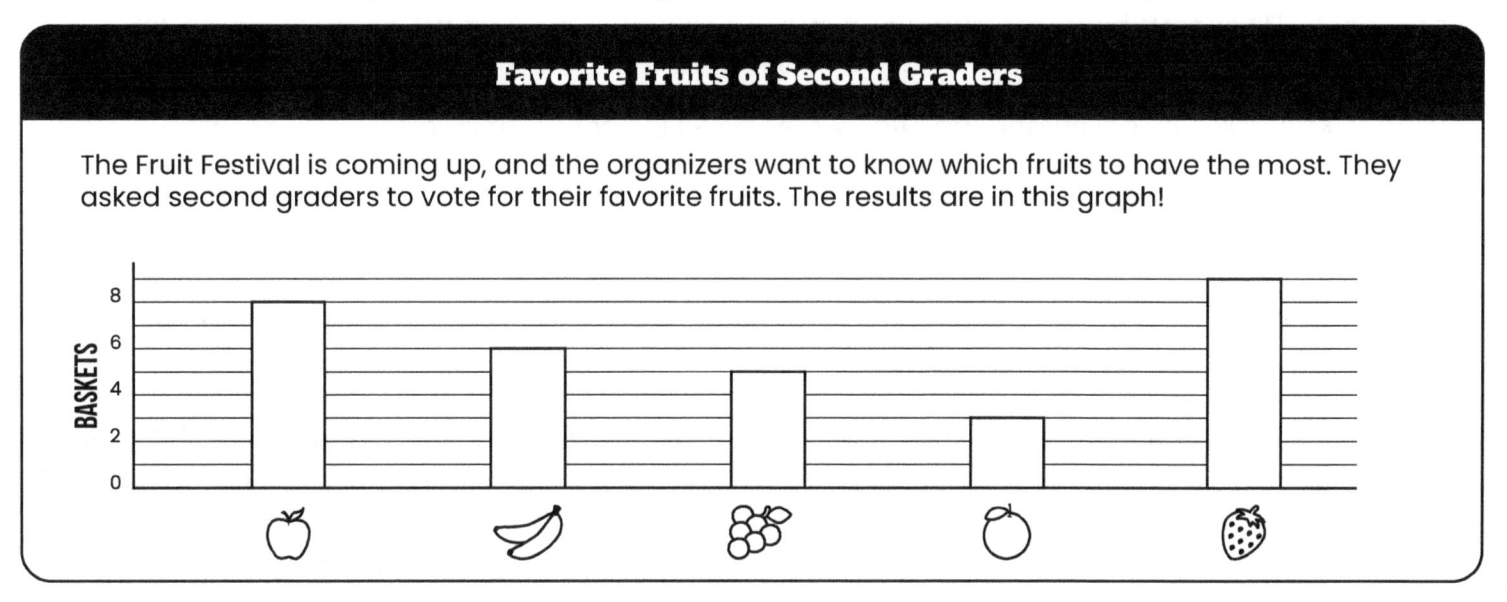

Favorite Fruits of Second Graders

The Fruit Festival is coming up, and the organizers want to know which fruits to have the most. They asked second graders to vote for their favorite fruits. The results are in this graph!

BASKETS: apple 8, banana 6, grapes 5, orange 3, strawberry 9

1 Which fruit will be the star of the Fruit Festival?
_____

2 If you were organizing the festival, how many baskets of oranges would you prepare?
_____

Now draw your own fruit stand for the festival!
What fruit would you sell? How would you decorate your stand?

Great Job, Graph Guru!

Activity 53 **Unit 3** CCSS: RL.2.3, RL.2.9

Character Comparison Adventure

Space Garden

Jake and Karina are siblings with big dreams and different interests. Jake is fascinated by the stars and planets. He spends hours reading about space and hopes to be an astronaut one day. He's always full of questions about the universe. Karina, his younger sister, loves exploring the world of nature. She has a collection of books about animals and plants and dreams of becoming a biologist. Karina is very observant and often writes notes in her nature journal.

One sunny day, they decided to combine their interests and create a 'Space Garden'. Jake researched plants that could grow in space, while Karina found ways to plant them using her knowledge of biology.

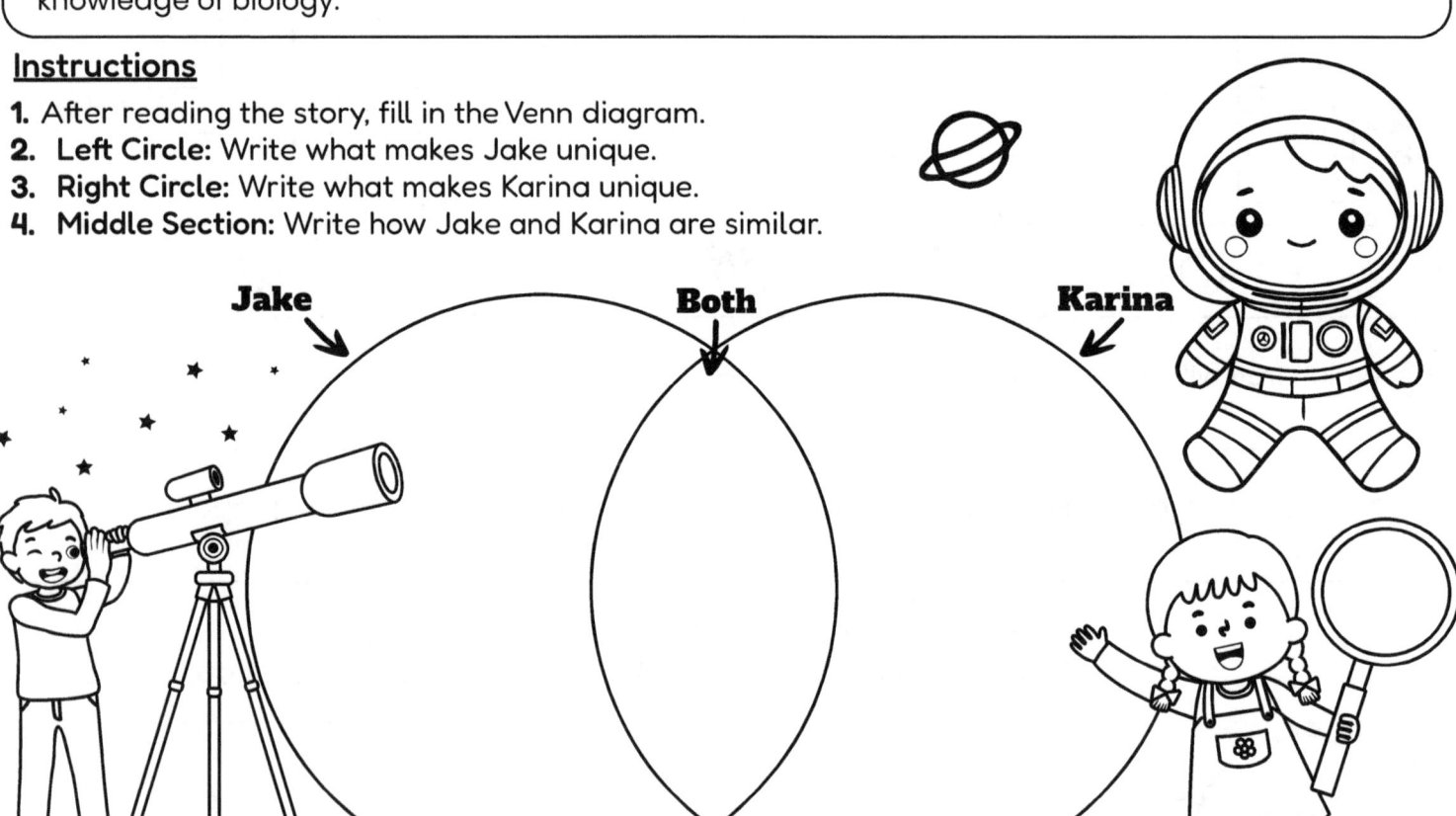

Instructions

1. After reading the story, fill in the Venn diagram.
2. **Left Circle:** Write what makes Jake unique.
3. **Right Circle:** Write what makes Karina unique.
4. **Middle Section:** Write how Jake and Karina are similar.

Jake   **Both**   **Karina**

Write a couple of sentences about what you like to explore, just like Jake and Karina.

_____

_____

Keep Up The Great Work!

Activity 54 — Unit 3 — CCSS: RI.2.5, RI.2.7

Whale of a Text Feature Adventure

Instructions

1. Let's learn about whales and discover different text features! Text features are parts of a text, like titles, pictures, captions, and fun facts, that help you understand the information better.
2. **Find and Circle:** As you read, look for different text features. Circle each one you find.
3. **Write and Explain:** After you find a text feature, write down what it is and why it is important.

- (1) **Title:** The name of the article.
- (2) **Picture:** An image that helps you see what you are reading about.
- (3) **Caption:** Words under a picture that tell you more about it.
- (4) **Fun Fact:** An interesting piece of information that stands out.

The Wonderful World of Whales

Whales are big, friendly animals that live in the ocean. They are like us in some ways because they are mammals. This means they breathe air, stay warm, and feed milk to their babies.

There are many kinds of whales. The Blue Whale is the biggest of them all. It's even bigger than the biggest dinosaurs! Another whale, the Beluga, is smaller and white. It lives in very cold water near the top of the world.

Whales are smart and can do many things. Humpback Whales are known for their songs. They make long, beautiful sounds that travel far under the water. Scientists think they sing to talk to each other or to find a mate.

Whales also travel a lot. They swim long distances every year to find food and to have their babies. The Gray Whale travels the farthest, going thousands of miles!

Whales help keep the ocean healthy. They eat lots of fish and small sea creatures. When whales die, their big bodies help make homes for creatures on the ocean floor.

Learning about whales helps us understand how special the ocean is. We need to take care of whales and the ocean for all the animals and people too.

This is a humpback whale. They are known for jumping high out of water!

Fun Fact
The Blue Whale is the biggest animal ever, even bigger than the biggest dinosaurs!

(1) What text features did you find in the story about whales?
_____
_____

(2) Why do you think each feature is used?
_____
_____

Great Job!

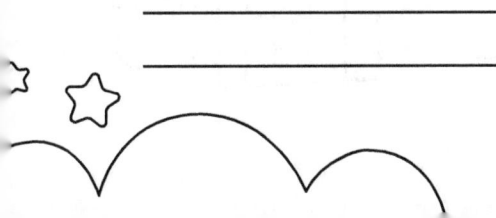

Activity 55 Unit 3 CCSS: RL.2.5, RL.2.2

Time Capsule Treasure Hunt

Instructions

1. Follow Lila and Ben as they uncover a secret in Lila's backyard.
2. **Map the Journey:** Think about the story's main events from start to finish.
   - **Beginning:** What starts the adventure?
   - **Middle:** What do Lila and Ben discover?
   - **End:** How does the story end with their discovery?

Lila found a mysterious key in her backyard. Excitedly, she showed it to her friend Ben, and they decided to find out what the key opened.

After searching high and low, they discovered a hidden door in the old garden shed. Inside, they found a chest filled with old toys and letters from the past.

They realized it was a time capsule from Lila's grandparents. Lila and Ben felt like they had traveled back in time.

Beginning

_____

Middle

_____

End

_____

Well Done!

Activity 56 — **Unit 3** — CCSS: RI.2.6, RL.2.6

Author's Purpose Pie

Instructions

1. **Decide the Purpose:** Think about why each statement was written – to share information, persuade, or entertain.
2. **Fill in the Pie:** Write the number of the statement in the correct section of the pie chart.

Example:
If you read, **"Brushing your teeth is important for keeping them healthy,"** think about why this was said. If it sounds like it's giving you information for your health, the purpose is to inform.

Statements

1. Eating vegetables is good for your health.
2. Long ago, in a kingdom filled with magic...
3. The sun is a star located at the center of our solar system.
4. Recycling helps keep our planet clean and healthy.
5. Once there was a silly puppy who loved adventures.
6. The first telephone was invented by Alexander Graham Bell in 1876.
7. You should eat more vegetables to stay healthy.
8. We must recycle to protect our environment.

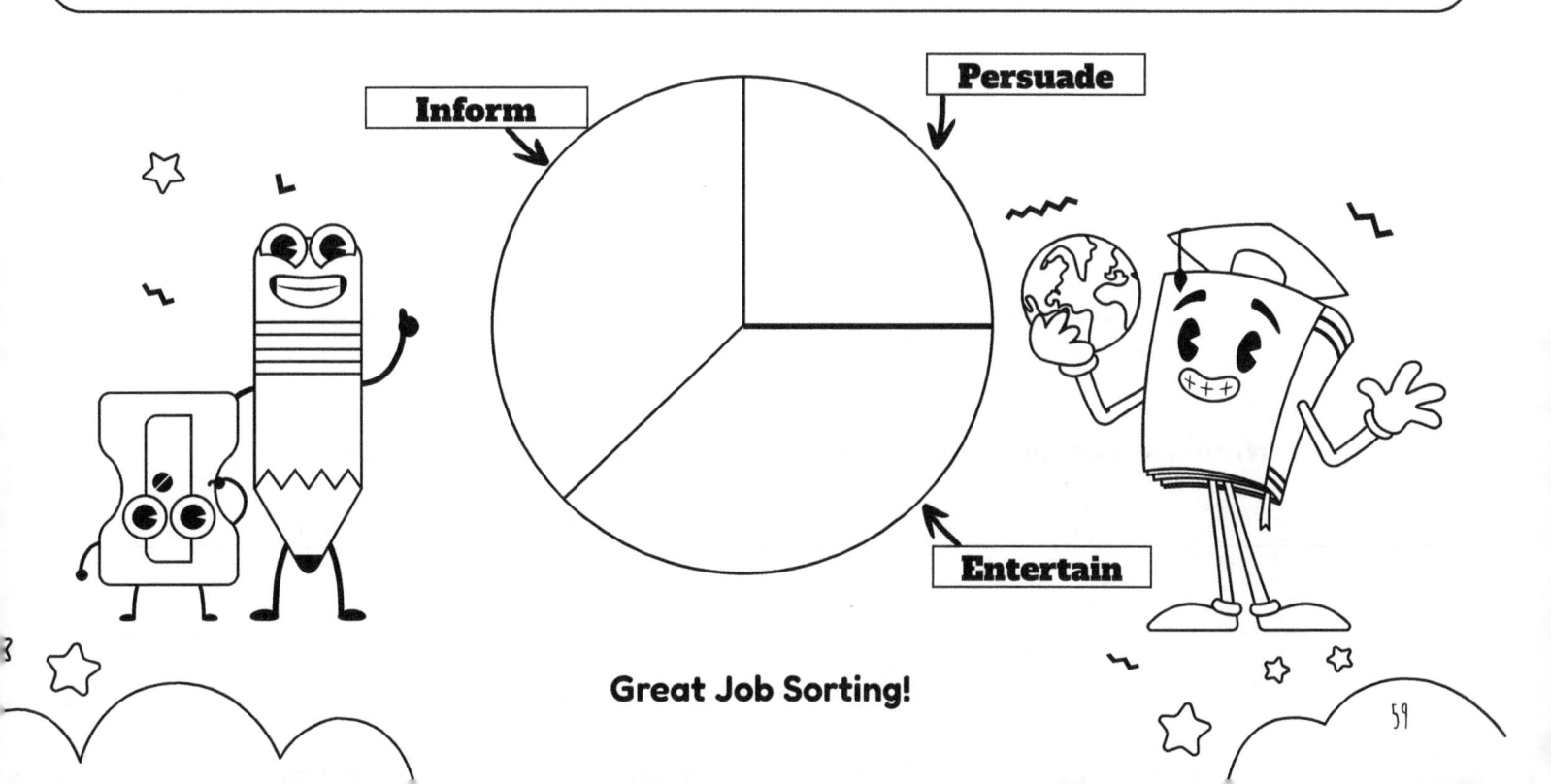

Inform — **Persuade** — **Entertain**

Great Job Sorting!

Activity 57 　　　　　**Unit 3**　　　　　CCSS: RL.2.7, RL.2.3

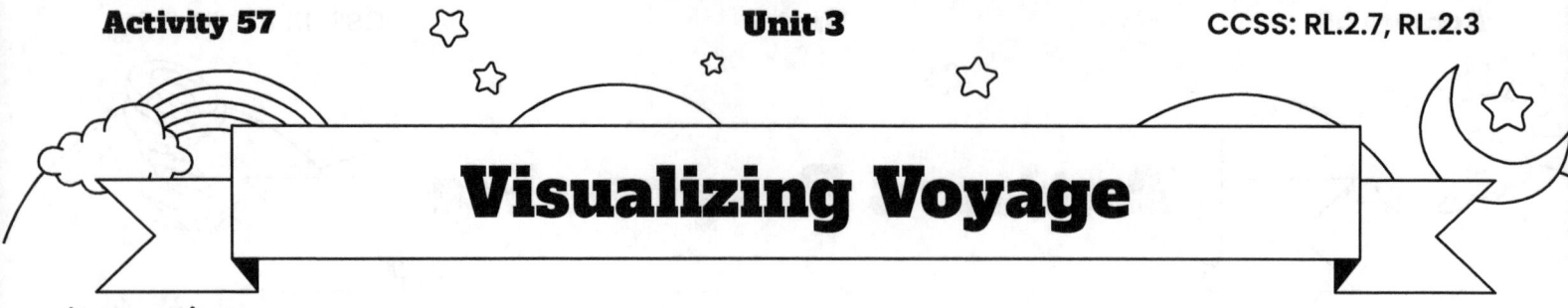

Visualizing Voyage

Instructions

Read the story below and imagine the scene described. In the easle below, draw what you see. Then, write a few sentences about your drawing, describing what is happening in it.

A Peaceful Forest

The forest was serene, with tall pine trees touching the blue sky. Birds sang sweetly, and a gentle stream bubbled nearby, reflecting the golden sunlight. In the distance, a majestic mountain stood proudly, its peak covered in snow.

Colorful flowers swayed in the breeze along the stream. A family of deer quietly made their way through the forest, stopping to drink from the stream. Nearby, squirrels chased each other up and down the trees, adding lively sounds.

As the sun set, the sky turned pink and orange, casting a warm glow over the peaceful forest.

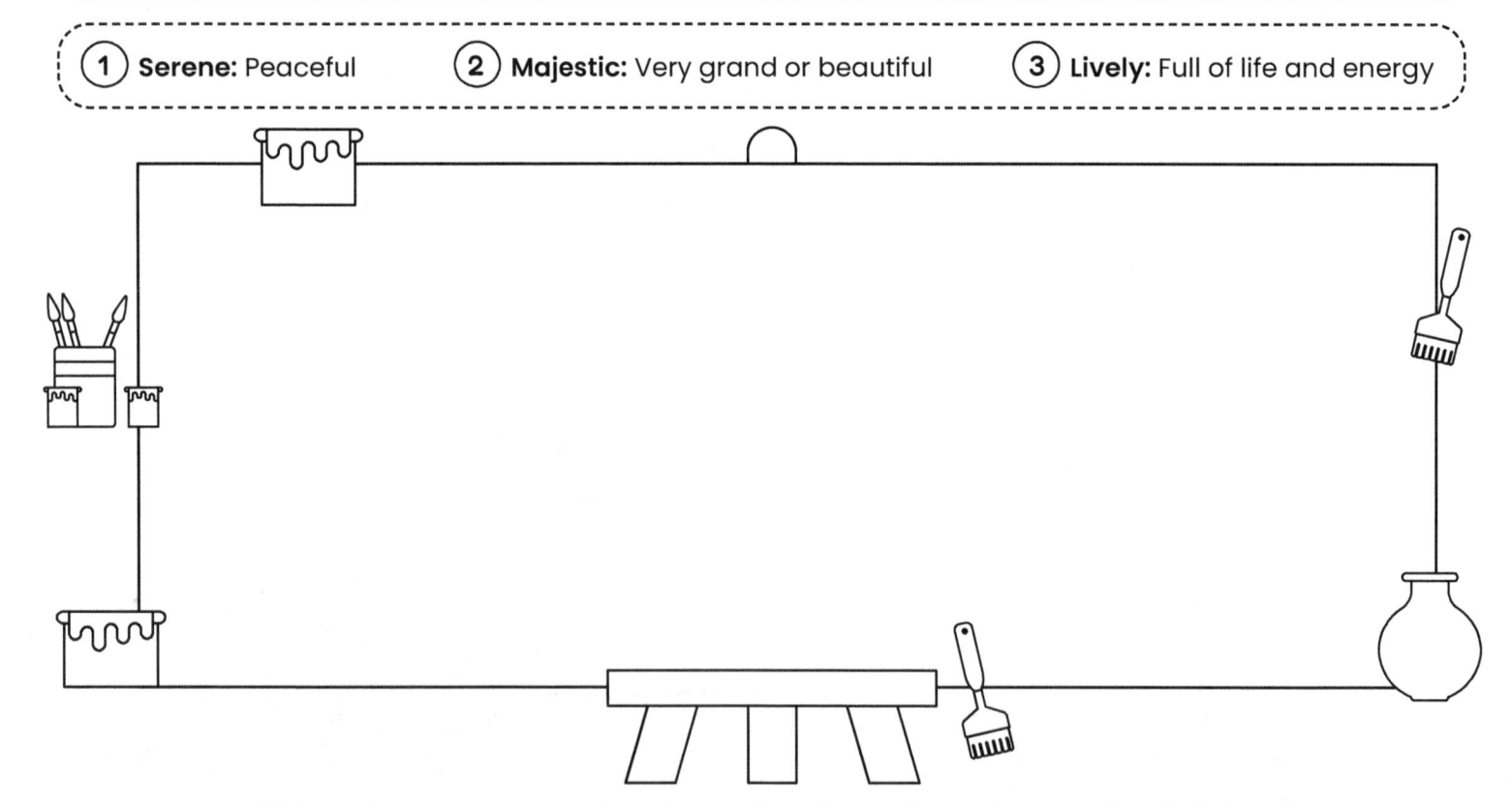

(1) **Serene:** Peaceful　　(2) **Majestic:** Very grand or beautiful　　(3) **Lively:** Full of life and energy

Write a few sentences about your drawing. What's happening in it?

_____

_____

Your Creativity Shines Bright!

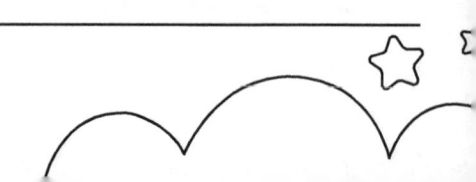

Activity 58 — Unit 3 — CCSS: RL.2.6, SL.2.1

Point of View

Instructions

1. **Read Each Scene:** Picture yourself in the story.
2. **Act It Out:** In your mind, play out the scene. What does it feel like to be in the story?
3. **Decide Who's Talking:** Write down who you think is telling the story for each scene.

Scene 1

I watched as my little brother tried to build a sandcastle. He was getting frustrated, but I gave him some tips and soon, we had a grand castle standing tall.

Scene 2

The day was hot, and I wished for some shade. I observed many children playing beneath me, laughing and having fun. They looked so tiny from up here.

Who is telling the story in Scene 1?

_____

Who is telling the story in Scene 2?

_____

You're A Great Story Explorer!

Activity 59   Unit 3   CCSS: RI.2.4, L.2.5

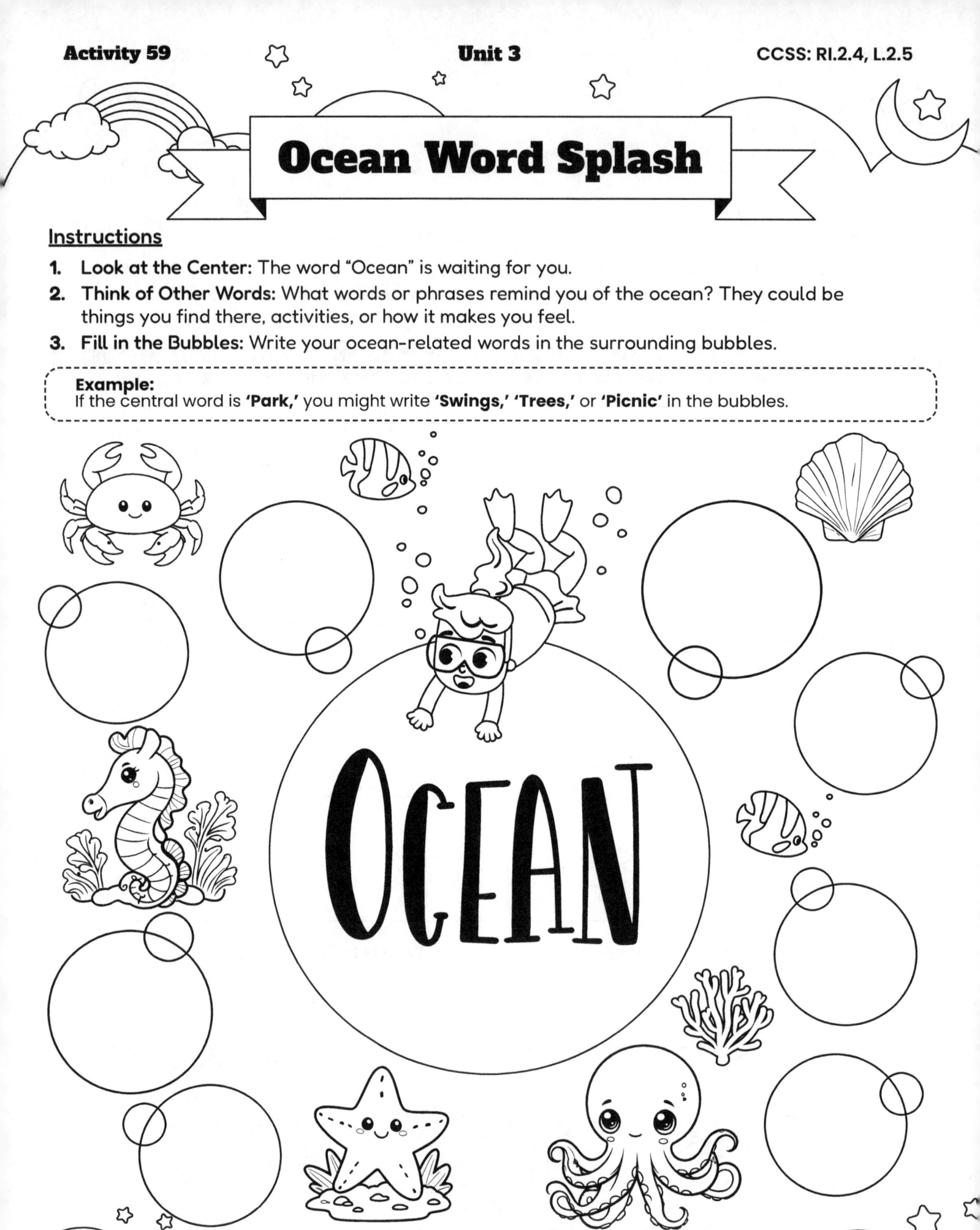

Ocean Word Splash

Instructions

1. **Look at the Center:** The word "Ocean" is waiting for you.
2. **Think of Other Words:** What words or phrases remind you of the ocean? They could be things you find there, activities, or how it makes you feel.
3. **Fill in the Bubbles:** Write your ocean-related words in the surrounding bubbles.

Example:
If the central word is **'Park,'** you might write **'Swings,' 'Trees,'** or **'Picnic'** in the bubbles.

You're A Word Explorer!

Activity 60 — **Unit 3** — CCSS: RL.2.2, RL.2.7

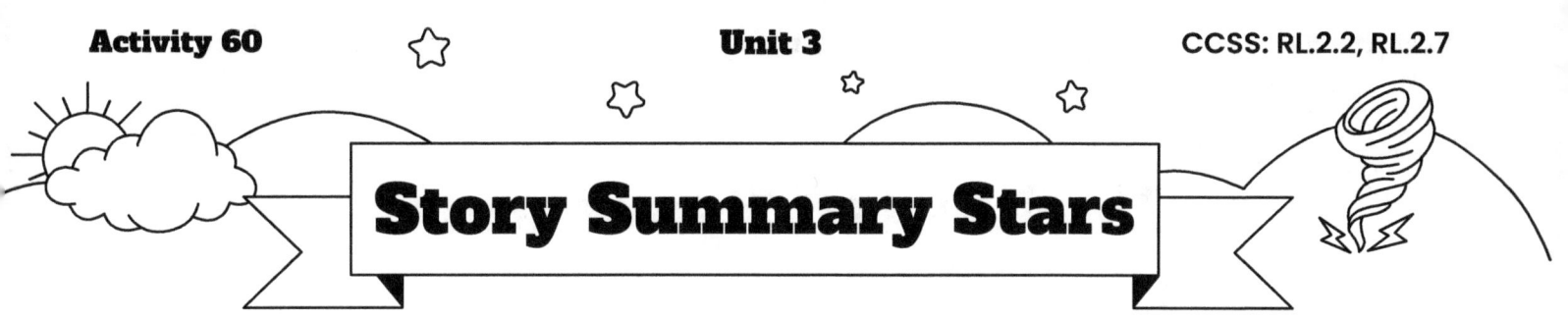

Story Summary Stars

Instructions

Let's become authors and artists for a day! After reading the story about Bella and her space adventure, show and tell us what happened.

> **Example:**
> If you read a story about a dog saving the day, you might draw the dog in the star and write about how the dog helped.

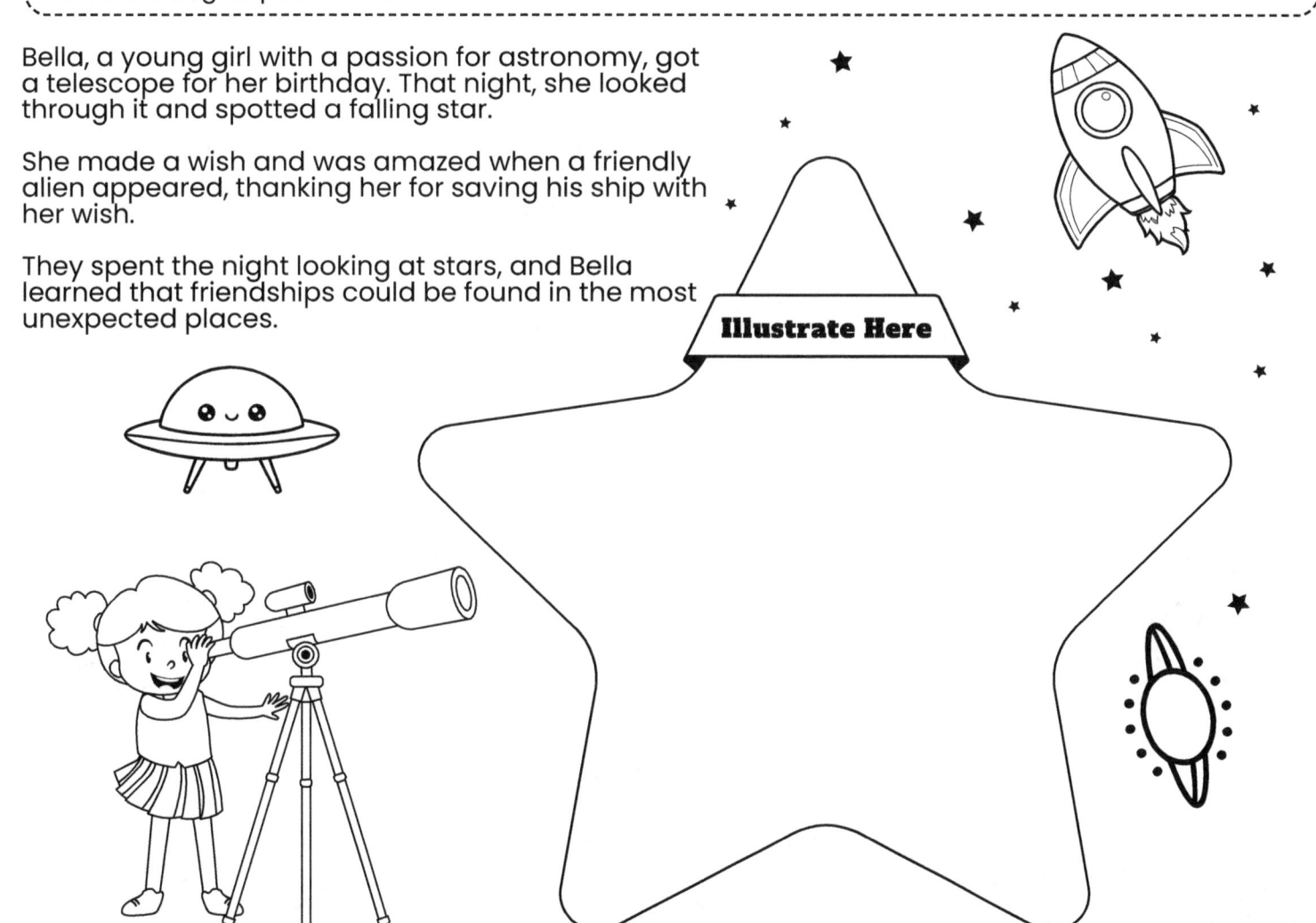

Bella, a young girl with a passion for astronomy, got a telescope for her birthday. That night, she looked through it and spotted a falling star.

She made a wish and was amazed when a friendly alien appeared, thanking her for saving his ship with her wish.

They spent the night looking at stars, and Bella learned that friendships could be found in the most unexpected places.

Illustrate Here

Write a few sentences to summarize the story. What happened, and what was the most special part?

_____

_____

_____

You're A Storytelling Star!

Activity 61 — **Unit 4** — CCSS: L.2.4a, L.2.5b

Enchanted Synonyms

Instructions
Read the story about Merlin and his friends in the enchanted forest. Then, find the synonym for each word in the Wizard's Word List. Write the matching letter from the Enchanted Synonyms. Don't forget to color the images!

The Wizard's Word Adventure

Merlin the wizard lived in a cozy treehouse filled with magical books and potions. One sunny day, he decided to teach his forest friends about the magic of words. He gathered them and said, "Today, we will find the perfect matches for some special words."

Merlin showed his friends a list of words: "happy," "quick," "bright," "move," "quiet," and "hard." Excited, the friends began their quest. As they explored, they saw cheerful birds, fast rabbits, and shiny fireflies. They noticed how quietly the owl moved and how tough it was to climb a steep hill. With each discovery, they felt the magic grow stronger.

Wizard's Word List

1. Happy _____
2. Quick _____
3. Bright _____
4. Move _____
5. Quiet _____
6. Hard _____

Enchanted Synonyms

A) Speedy
B) Cheerful
C) Luminous
D) Shift
E) Silent
F) Difficult

You've Matched With Magical Precision!

Activity 62 **Unit 4** CCSS: RI.2.4, L.2.5

Synonym Search

Instructions

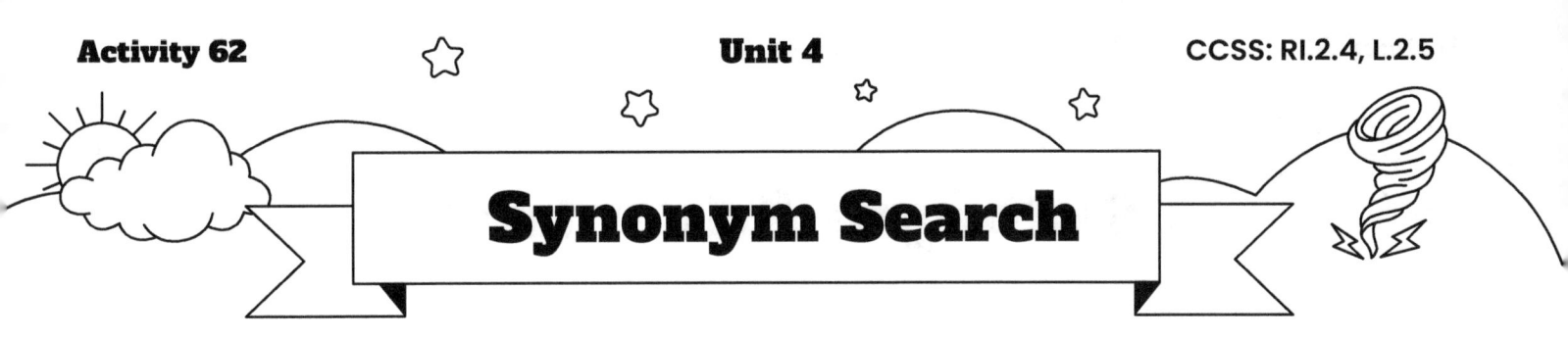

Read the short story about Tom the detective, then match each word from the Words List to its synonym by drawing a line between them. After matching, write a sentence using each synonym to show you understand what it means. Don't forget to color the images!

The Synonym Detective's Adventure

Tom the detective loved finding matching words. One sunny morning, he listed some words he found in a book. Tom decided to find their matching pairs in the enchanted forest. As he explored, he saw friendly animals, cold streams, tiny bugs, brave knights, giggling fairies, and tired travelers. Tom knew he had to find the right synonyms to complete his mission.

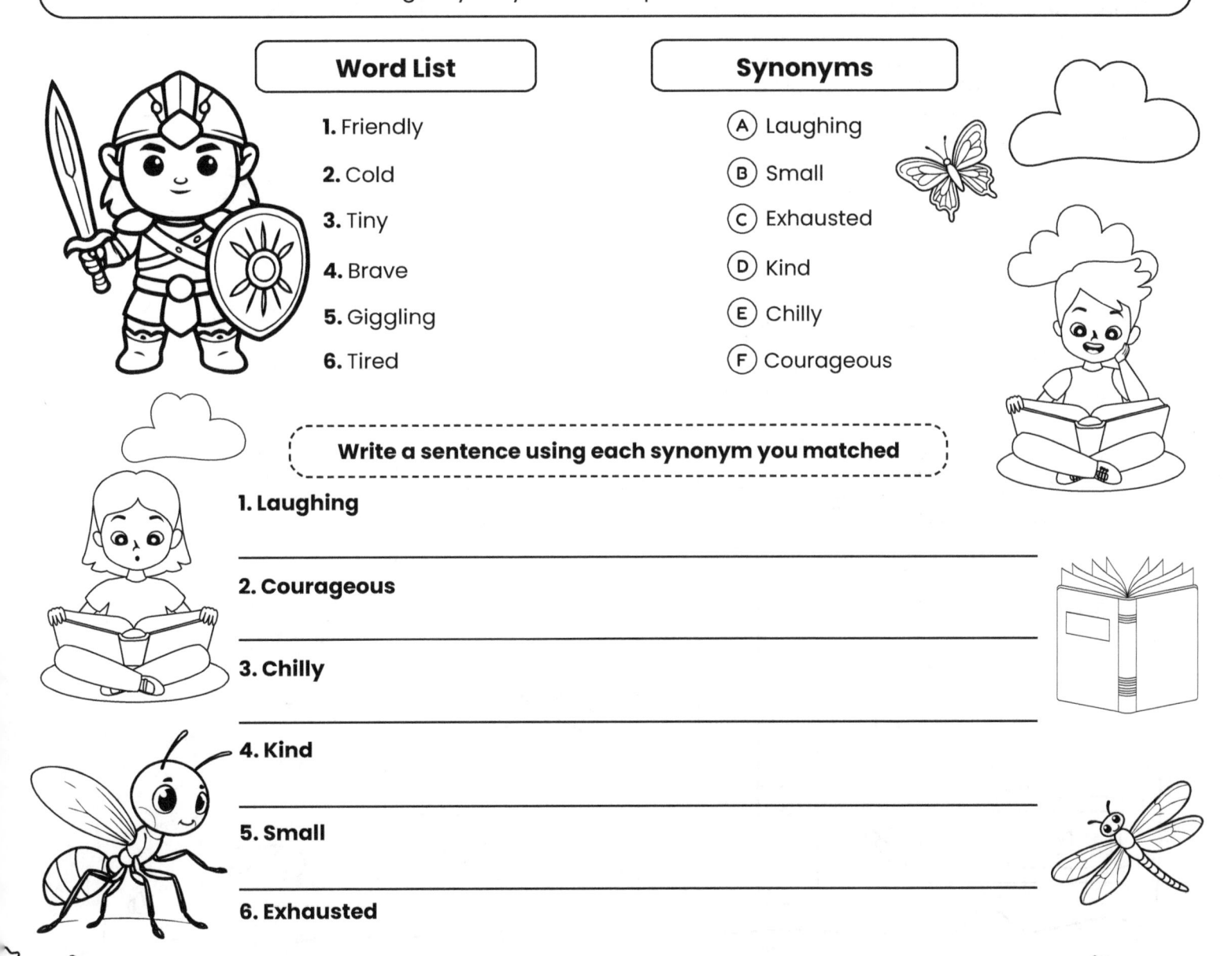

Word List

1. Friendly
2. Cold
3. Tiny
4. Brave
5. Giggling
6. Tired

Synonyms

A. Laughing
B. Small
C. Exhausted
D. Kind
E. Chilly
F. Courageous

Write a sentence using each synonym you matched

1. Laughing
_____

2. Courageous
_____

3. Chilly
_____

4. Kind
_____

5. Small
_____

6. Exhausted
_____

You're A Synonym Superstar!

Activity 63 Unit 4 CCSS: L.2.4a, L.2.5b

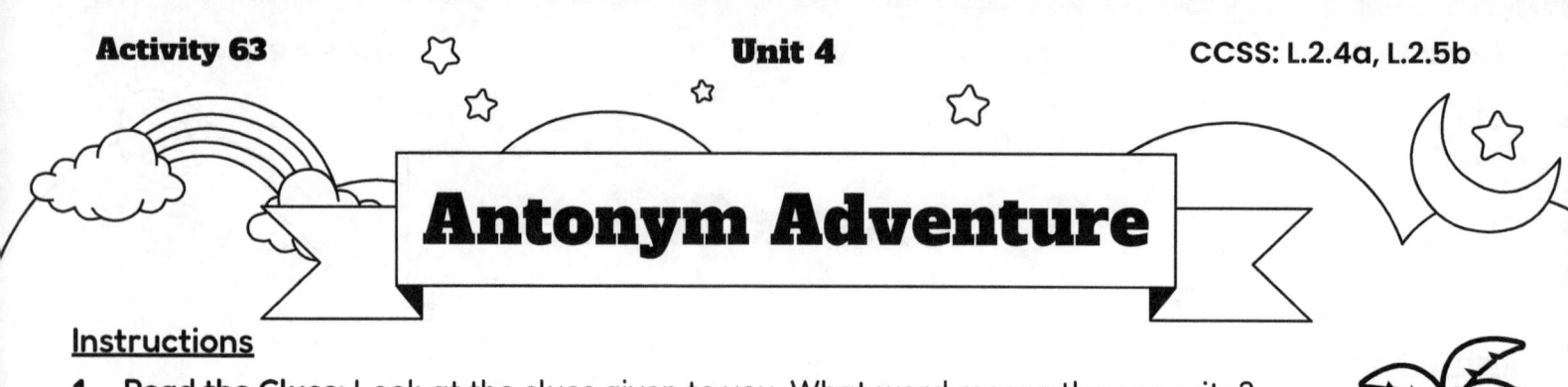

Antonym Adventure

Instructions
1. **Read the Clues:** Look at the clues given to you. What word means the opposite?
2. **Find the Antonym:** Think of the antonym (opposite word) that answers each clue.
3. **Complete the Puzzle:** Write your ocean-related words in the surrounding bubbles.

Example:
If the clue is 'Hot,' the antonym you write might be 'Cold.'

Mia and Max

Mia and Max loved spending afternoons at the city park. One sunny day, they found a full playground with lots of children playing. The bright sun made everything look cheerful. They walked along the path and felt the smooth stones under their feet. Suddenly, they came across a weak branch that had fallen from a tree. They heard a happy dog barking and saw it running around joyfully. Their day at the park was always full of new discoveries and fun.

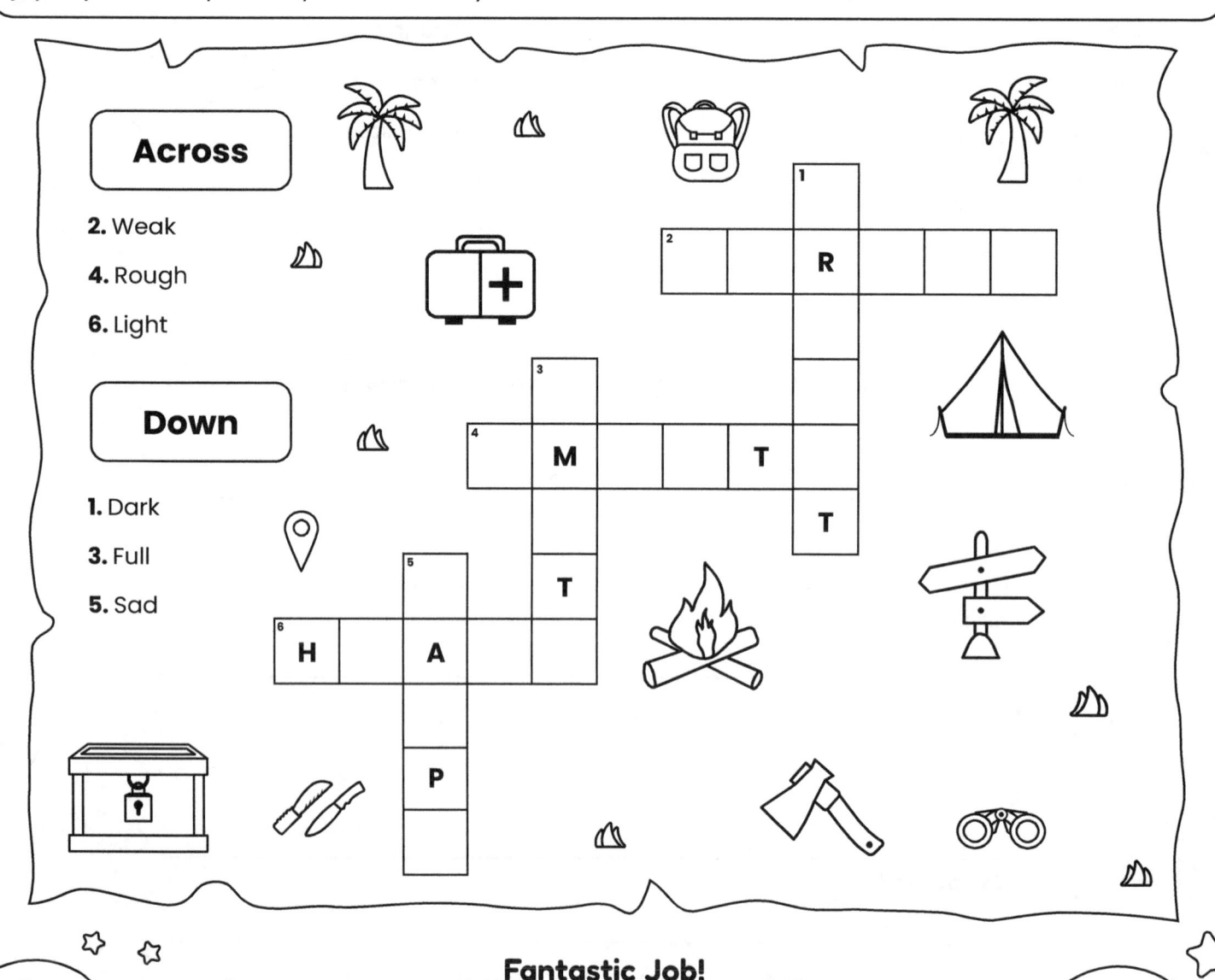

Across
2. Weak
4. Rough
6. Light

Down
1. Dark
3. Full
5. Sad

Fantastic Job!

Activity 64 — **Unit 4** — CCSS: RI.2.4, L.2.5

Prefix Park

Emma and Ben

In Prefix Park, everyone was happy playing games. But one day, Emma felt unhappy because she lost her favorite toy. Ben, who was always kind, tried to cheer her up. They decided to replay the game they loved, and Emma felt better. They realized that being unkind to each other would never help, so they always stayed cheerful and kind.

Instructions

1. **Identify the Words:** In the story above, underline the words with prefixes.
2. **Match the Words:** Look at the Root Words list and match each to its new meaning by writing the letter of its matching new meaning beside it.

Root Words

1. Happy _____
2. Kind _____
3. Like _____
4. Play _____

Prefix Options

A. Unlike – not similar to
B. Unkind – not kind
C. Replay – to play again
D. Unhappy – not happy

1) Why was Emma unhappy?
_____

2) What did Ben do to help Emma feel better?
_____

3) Why is it important to be kind?
_____

You're A Word Wizard In Prefix Park!

Activity 65 **Unit 4** CCSS: L.2.4c, L.2.4d

Suffix Safari

Instructions

1. **Start with Base Words:** Look at the words we're starting with on the left side of the page.
2. **Choose Your Suffix:** Think about whether '**-ed**', '**-ing**', '**-er**', or '**-est**' fits best to finish our sentences.
3. **Complete the Sentences:** Fill in the blanks with your newly formed words.

Example:
If 'jump' is the base word, for 'He is _____ high,' you add '-ing' to make 'jumping'.

Mia and Max

One sunny day, a group of friends visited a safari park. They played games and helped each other spot different animals. Sarah helped her friend Tom find a quick path to the lion's den. They were the happiest when they saw the playful monkeys. By the end of the day, everyone agreed it was the quickest and most exciting adventure they had ever had.

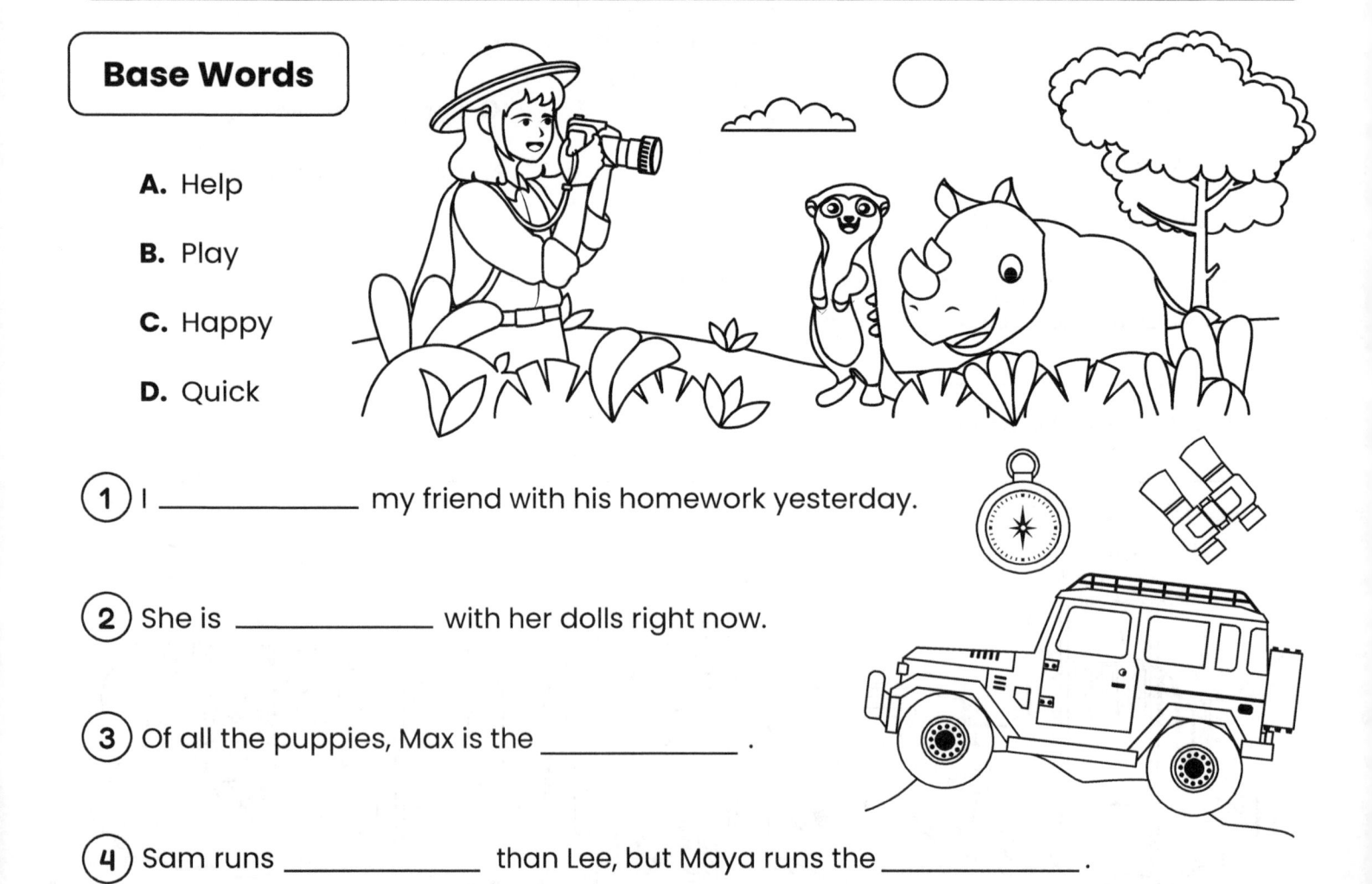

Base Words

A. Help

B. Play

C. Happy

D. Quick

1) I _____ my friend with his homework yesterday.

2) She is _____ with her dolls right now.

3) Of all the puppies, Max is the _____ .

4) Sam runs _____ than Lee, but Maya runs the _____ .

Great Job, Explorer!

Activity 66 — **Unit 4** — CCSS: L.2.4a, L.2.1e

Homophone Hunt

What are homophones? Homophones are tricky words that sound the same but have different meanings.

Instructions
1. **Read the Story:** Follow along and circle the correct word in each sentence.
2. **Fill in the Blanks:** Then below fill in the blanks with the correct homophones.

Mia and Max

One sunny day, Detective Dog and his son decided to go on a big adventure. They were excited to see the beautiful sea and write about their discoveries. As they walked along the beach, Detective Dog said, "The (**sun / son**) is shining brightly today." His son replied, "I can't wait to (**sea / see**) the ocean!"

Detective Dog asked his son to (**write / right**) his name in the sand. "Please (**write / right**) your name on the beach," he said. His son smiled and wrote his name. Then, they saw a group of kids playing with apples. "She (**ate / eight**) apples for a week," said one of the kids. Detective Dog laughed and said, "That sounds like a fun challenge!"

1. The _____ is shining brightly today.
2. Please _____ your name on your paper.
3. I can't wait to _____ the ocean.
4. She _____ apples for a week.

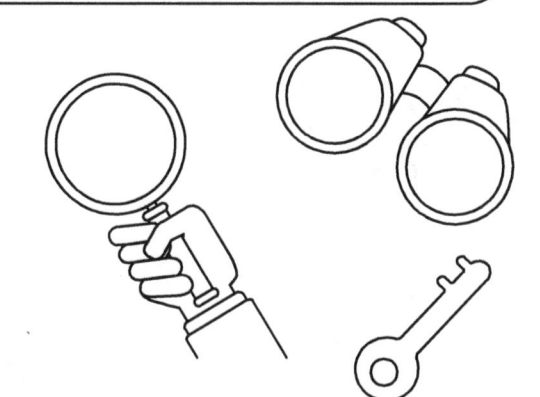

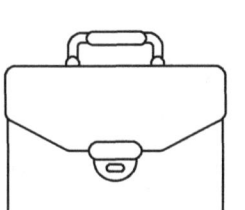

You are so smart! Circle the correct homophone in each sentence below!

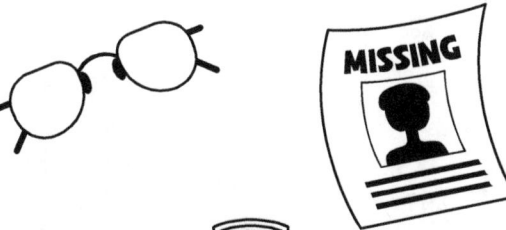

5. The (blue / blew) balloon floated away.
6. He (knew / new) the answer to the question.
7. She likes to (buy / by) new books to read.
8. The (pair / pear) of shoes was under the bed.

Awesome Job, Detective!

Activity 67   Unit 4   CCSS: L.2.4c, L.2.4d

Root Word Rally

Instructions

1. **Read the Story:** Read the story below to understand how words can grow and change.
2. **Find the Root Word:** Look at the root word at the bottom of the tree.
3. **Think of New Words:** Use the prefixes and suffixes provided to create new words from the root words.
4. **Write on the Lines:** Write the new words on the branches growing from the root word.

Example:
If "read" is the root word, you might write "reader" or "reading" on the branches.

Prefixes & Suffixes	The Magical Tree
un- re- -er -est -ing -ed	In a quiet forest, there was a magical tree that helped words grow. One day, Alex and Mia discovered the tree. It had root words at the base, and as they watched, branches grew with new words. Alex saw the root word "play" turn into "playing" and "played." Mia saw "happy" become "happier" and "happiest." They realized they could make many new words by adding different beginnings and endings. Excited, they wrote down the root words and thought of all the new words they could create. The magical tree taught them that with a little change, words could grow and change, too.

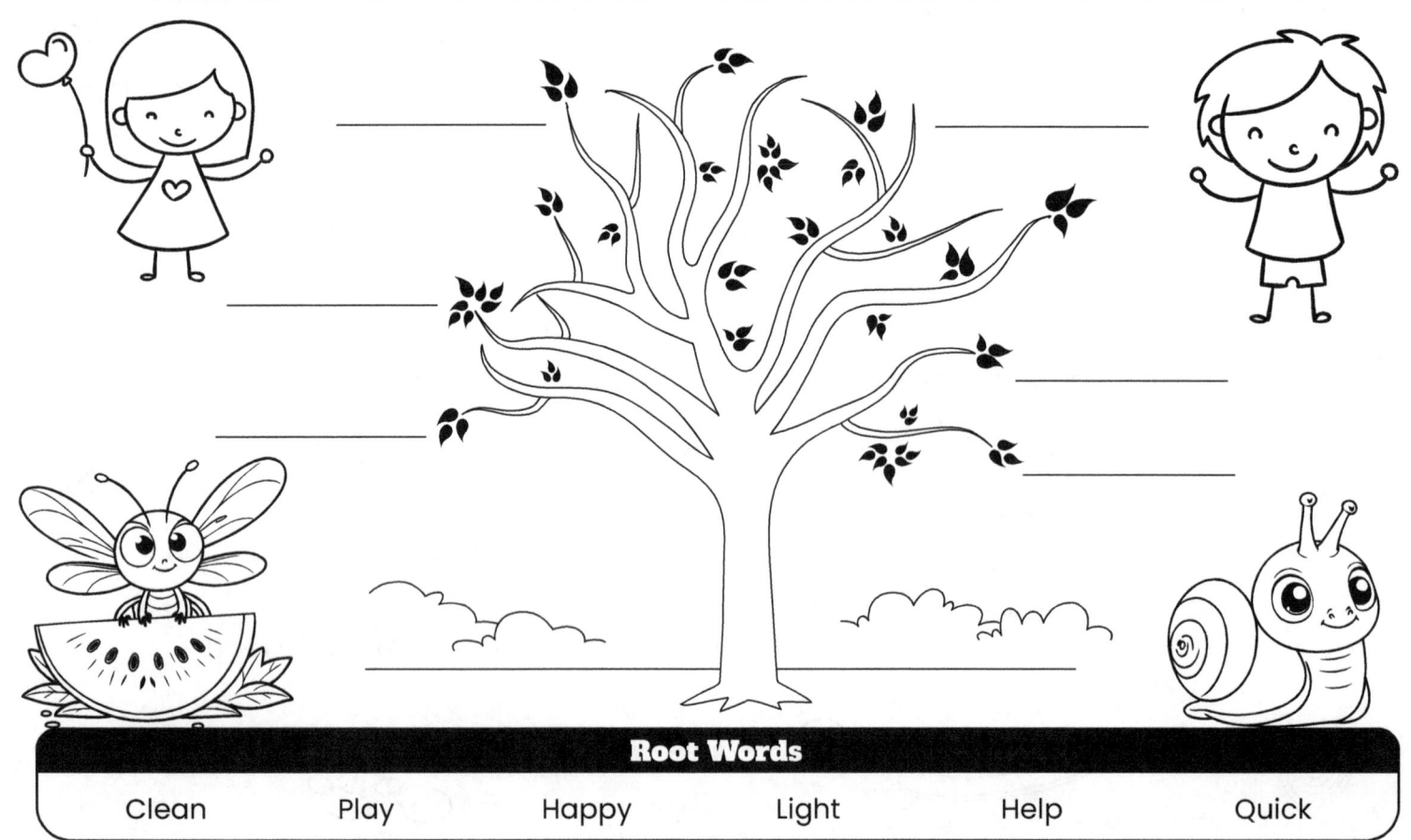

Root Words

Clean   Play   Happy   Light   Help   Quick

You're Doing Great! Keep It Up!

Activity 68 Unit 4 CCSS: L.2.5a, L.2.6

Word Category Camp

Instructions

1. **Read the Story:** As you read the story notice how the words are used.
2. **Fill in the Blanks:** Look at the words scattered around the page and think about which category each word belongs to.
3. **Write the Words:** Write each word in the correct tent where it belongs.

A Day at Word Category Camp

One sunny day, the campers at Word Category Camp went on a fun adventure. First, they saw a big, friendly dog playing with a ball near the tents. Then, they walked to the garden and picked a fresh, orange carrot and a juicy tomato for their lunch. After eating, they visited the school tent to learn about different places and read books from the library tent. They also met a wise elephant who taught them about sorting words into categories. The campers had so much fun learning and exploring that they couldn't wait to come back the next day.

DOG ELEPHANT CARROT LIBRARY TOMATO SCHOOL

Animals   Foods   Places

_____   _____   _____
_____   _____   _____

1) Who was playing with a ball near the tents?
_____

2) Where did the campers go to learn about different places?
_____

3) Who taught the campers about sorting words into categories?
_____

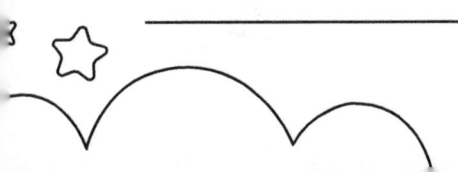

Great work!

Activity 69 — **Unit 4** — CCSS: L.2.4a, L.2.5b

Idiom Island

Instructions
1. **Read the Story:** As you read the story notice how the idioms are used.
2. **Draw the Literal Meaning:** In the first box, draw a picture showing the literal meaning of the idiom (exactly what the words say).
3. **Draw the Figurative Meaning:** In the second box, draw a picture showing the figurative meaning of the idiom (what the phrase really means).

A Place of Fun and Surprises

One sunny day, Lily and Max visited Idiom Island, a place full of fun and surprises. As they walked along the beach, it started raining cats and dogs. They quickly found shelter under a big palm tree. "This weather is a piece of cake compared to the storm we had last week," Max said. Later, they found a treasure chest. When they opened it, Max let the cat out of the bag and revealed the secret hiding place to everyone. To end the day, they played a game where they had to hit the nail on the head with a hammer. They had a fantastic adventure on Idiom Island!

Idioms	Literal Meaning	Figurative Meaning
It's raining cats and dogs.		
A piece of cake.		
Let the cat out of the bag.		
Hit the nail on the head.		

You're An Idiom Master!

Activity 70 — **Unit 4** — CCSS: L.2.5b, L.2.1e

Shades of Meaning Mountain

Instructions

1. **Read the Excerpts:** Read each short excerpt to understand how words can have different levels of intensity.
2. **Climb the Mountain:** Look at the word groups below. Decide which word is the least intense and which is the most intense.
3. **Place the Words:** Write the words on the mountain drawing provided, from the bottom (least intense) to the top (most intense word).

Passage 1:
When Lily spoke to her little brother, she often **whispered** so she wouldn't wake the baby. Sometimes, she would just **talk** quietly if they were in the living room. But when they were outside playing, she could **yell** as loud as she wanted.

Yell, Whisper, Talk

Passage 2:
On a cool morning, Jack felt **warm** in his jacket as he walked to school. By lunchtime, the sun made it feel **hot** outside. During summer, the temperatures could get so high that it felt like they were **boiling**.

Hot, Warm, Boiling

Passage 3:
Ella felt a bit **nervous** about her first day at a new school. When she entered the classroom, she was more **scared** than she expected. By the time the teacher asked her to introduce herself, she was downright **terrified**.

Terrified, Nervous, Scared

Keep Climbing!

Activity 71 — Unit 4 — CCSS: L.2.4d, L.2.4a

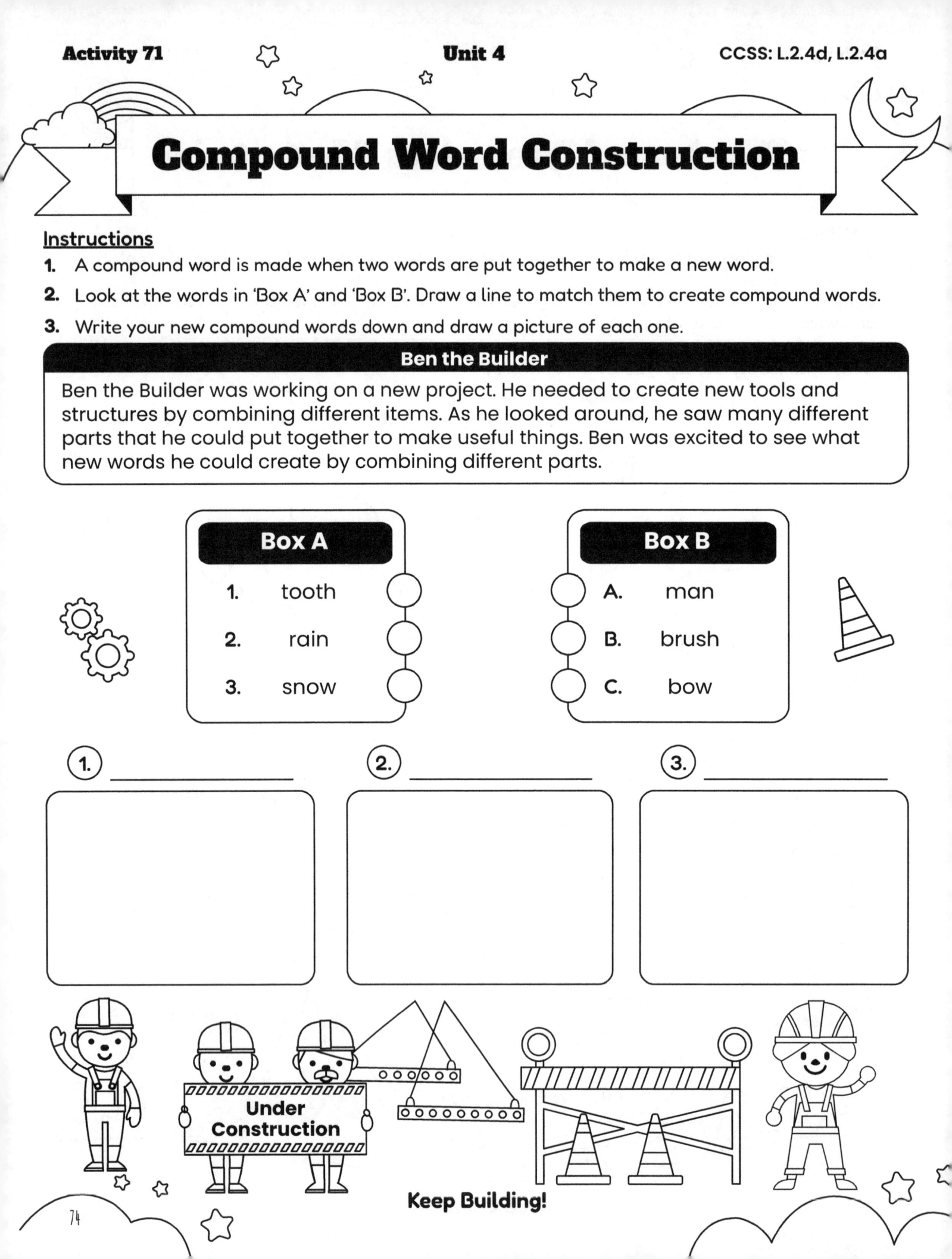

Compound Word Construction

Instructions

1. A compound word is made when two words are put together to make a new word.
2. Look at the words in 'Box A' and 'Box B'. Draw a line to match them to create compound words.
3. Write your new compound words down and draw a picture of each one.

Ben the Builder

Ben the Builder was working on a new project. He needed to create new tools and structures by combining different items. As he looked around, he saw many different parts that he could put together to make useful things. Ben was excited to see what new words he could create by combining different parts.

Box A
1. tooth
2. rain
3. snow

Box B
A. man
B. brush
C. bow

1. _____
2. _____
3. _____

Keep Building!

74

Activity 72 **Unit 4** CCSS: L.2.6, L.2.3a

Vocabulary Story Studio

Instructions

1. **Read the Beginning:** Start with the story beginning provided below.
2. **Continue the Story:** Write a story that includes all the vocabulary words. Be as creative as you want!
3. **Underline the Words:** Remember to underline each vocabulary word you use in your story.

Story Starter!
One sunny day, I found a shiny key in my backyard. When I turned the key, a hidden door opened. Behind the door, I saw a bright light and heard a voice whisper, 'Your adventure starts now.' I took a deep breath and stepped inside...

Vocabulary Words

Adventure   Treasure   Brave
Whispered   Rainbow

Fantastic Job!

Activity 73 — **Unit 4** — CCSS: L.2.4a, SL.2.2

Context Clue Cinema

Instructions

1. Read the sentences below.
2. Each sentence uses a vocabulary word in a way that helps you understand what it means.
3. Write your own sentence for each word, using clues to show what the word means.

Glimmer

Example: The stars began to glimmer in the night sky, shining softly.

_____
_____
_____

Rustle

Example: I heard a rustle in the bushes, like leaves being moved by the wind.

_____
_____
_____

Dart

Example: The cat would dart across the room, moving so fast you could barely see it.

_____
_____
_____

Ponder

Example: She would often ponder about the meaning of life, thinking deeply for hours.

_____
_____
_____

Soar

Example: The eagle would soar high above the mountains, gliding effortlessly through the air.

_____
_____
_____

You Are Excellent!

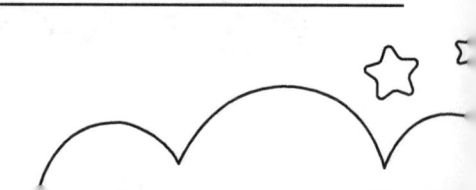

Activity 74   **Unit 4**   CCSS: L.2.5a, L.2.5b

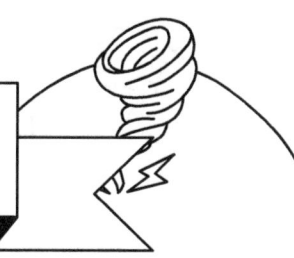

Word Relationship Road

Instructions

1. **Read the Story:** Follow along with the short story below to understand how words are connected.
2. **Look at the Words:** Check out the words scattered on your map.
3. **Make Connections:** Draw lines to connect words that go together. How many connections can you make?

A Day with Sammy's Animals

Sammy had a pet dog named Max. Every morning, Max would bark happily as Sammy got ready for school. On weekends, Sammy loved to visit the farm where they would see the cows mooing in the fields. Sammy also had a cat named Whiskers who loved to meow when she was hungry. In the evenings, Sammy enjoyed watching his fish swim in their tank. The animals always made Sammy's day special.

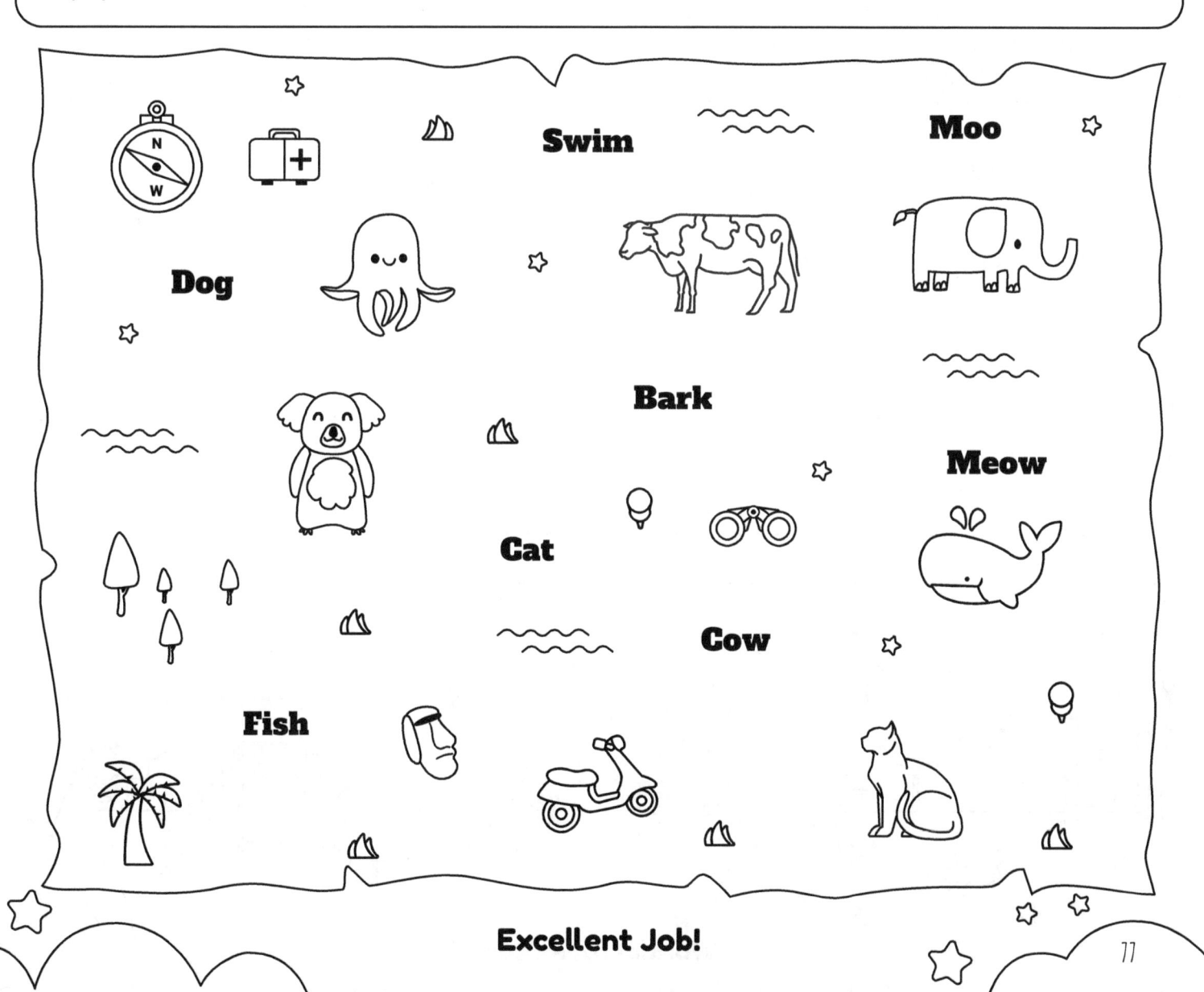

Swim   Moo

Dog

Bark

Meow

Cat

Cow

Fish

Excellent Job!

Activity 75 Unit 4 CCSS: L.2.4a, L.2.5b

Proverb Playground

Instructions
1. Look at the proverbs below.
2. Choose two and draw a picture for each to show what you think they mean.
3. Write a sentence explaining your drawing.

The Busy Playground

One sunny day, the playground was full of happy children. Sarah carefully saved her allowance for weeks to buy a new jump rope, remembering that a penny saved is a penny earned. She arrived at the playground early in the morning, knowing that the early bird catches the worm and she wanted to be the first on the swings.

While playing, Sarah accidentally spilled her juice. Instead of getting upset, she told herself, "Don't cry over spilled milk," and went to play on the slide. Later, there was a race among the kids. Some of them dashed off quickly, but Sarah took her time, remembering that slow and steady wins the race. In the end, she crossed the finish line with a big smile, proud of her steady effort.

- A penny saved is a penny earned.
- The early bird catches the worm.
- Don't cry over spilled milk.
- Slow and steady wins the race.

Wonderful Pictures!

Activity 76 Unit 4 CCSS: L.2.1e, L.2.6

Adjective Art Gallery

Instructions

1. Read the story below. Pay attention to how the adjectives are used to describe scenes and objects.
2. Look at the list of adjectives below.
3. For each adjective draw a scene or an object in the easel that shows what it means.

Example:
For **"Sparkling,"** you might draw a shining diamond or a starry night sky.

Adjective Adventure

In a magical forest, a tiny bird sang noisily on a bumpy road. Shay walked carefully, spotting a sparkling lake. Beside it stood a gigantic tree. She touched the rough bark and watched fish swim in the clear water. Suddenly, the tree spoke, 'Welcome, Shay.' Startled, she listened. 'Find the hidden treasure under the sparkling rock,' it said. Shay found the rock, lifted it, and discovered a tiny, glowing key. 'Your adventure has just begun,' whispered the tree.

Bumpy   **Sparkling**   **Gigantic**

Great imagination!

Activity 77 — **Unit 4** — CCSS: L.2.1d, SL.2.6

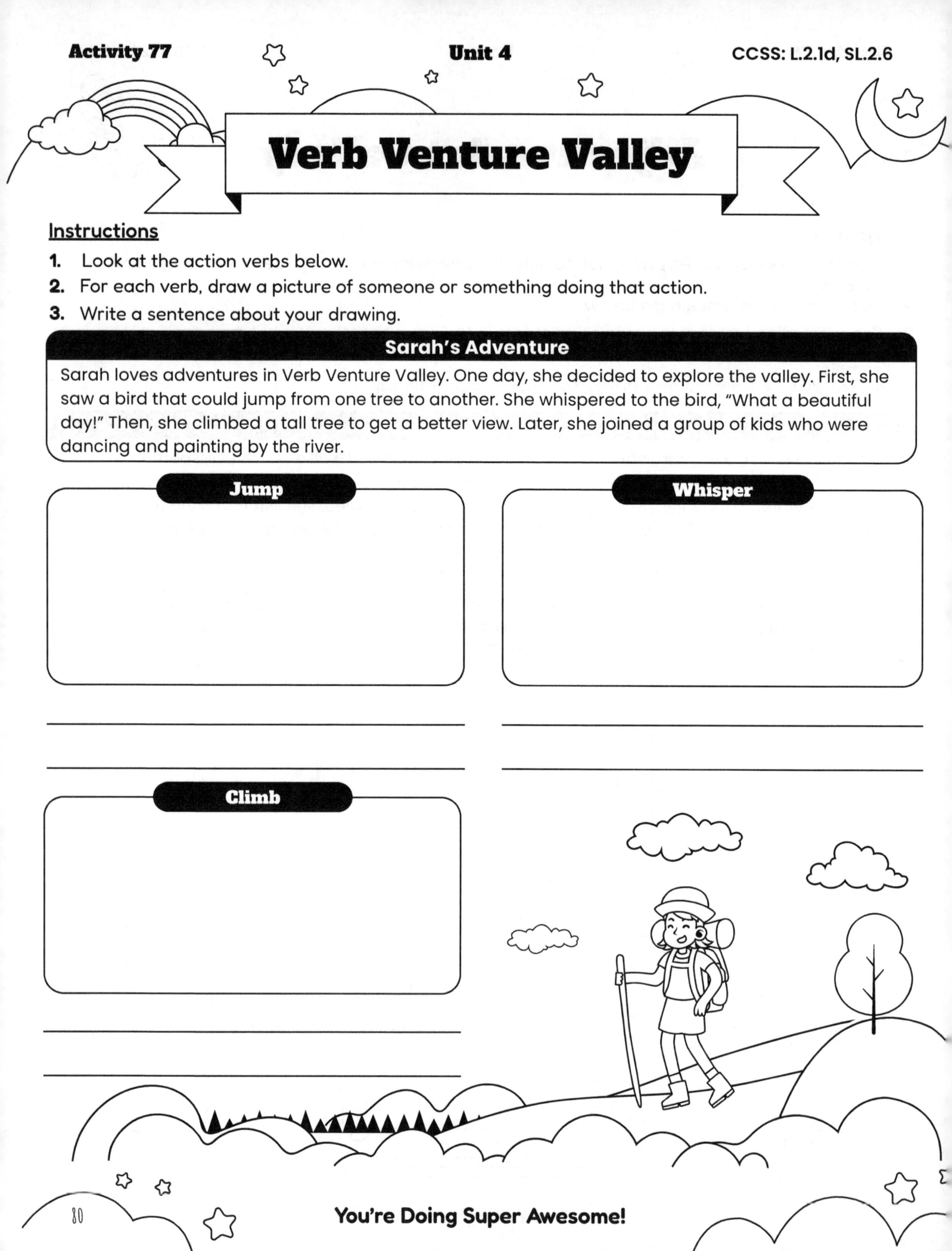

Verb Venture Valley

Instructions

1. Look at the action verbs below.
2. For each verb, draw a picture of someone or something doing that action.
3. Write a sentence about your drawing.

Sarah's Adventure

Sarah loves adventures in Verb Venture Valley. One day, she decided to explore the valley. First, she saw a bird that could jump from one tree to another. She whispered to the bird, "What a beautiful day!" Then, she climbed a tall tree to get a better view. Later, she joined a group of kids who were dancing and painting by the river.

Jump

Whisper

Climb

You're Doing Super Awesome!

Activity 78 — **Unit 4** — CCSS: L.2.5a, L.2.3a

Connotation Cafe

Instructions

1. Look at our special menu of words below.
2. For each word, write a sentence on the lines provided. Your sentence should show if the word feels happy (positive), sad (negative), or just okay (neutral).

Example:
For **"Bright,"** you might write: **"The bright sun made me feel warm and happy."**

MENU

1. Loud
   _____
2. Bright
   _____
3. Fast
   _____
4. Heavy
   _____
5. Quiet
   _____

You Are Impressive!

Activity 79 | **Unit 4** | **CCSS: L.2.1d, L.2.1e**

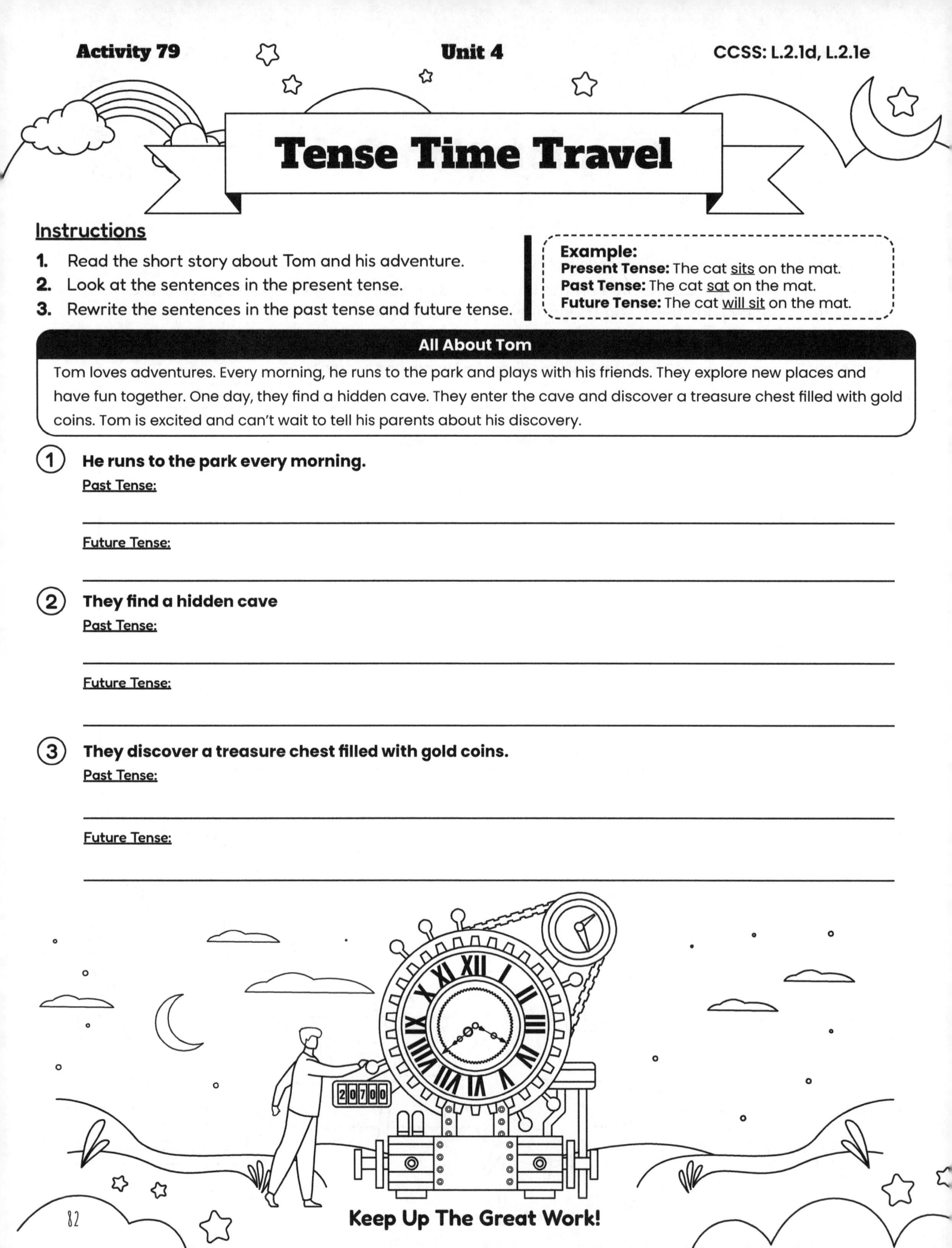

Tense Time Travel

Instructions

1. Read the short story about Tom and his adventure.
2. Look at the sentences in the present tense.
3. Rewrite the sentences in the past tense and future tense.

Example:
Present Tense: The cat sits on the mat.
Past Tense: The cat sat on the mat.
Future Tense: The cat will sit on the mat.

All About Tom

Tom loves adventures. Every morning, he runs to the park and plays with his friends. They explore new places and have fun together. One day, they find a hidden cave. They enter the cave and discover a treasure chest filled with gold coins. Tom is excited and can't wait to tell his parents about his discovery.

① **He runs to the park every morning.**
Past Tense: _____
Future Tense: _____

② **They find a hidden cave**
Past Tense: _____
Future Tense: _____

③ **They discover a treasure chest filled with gold coins.**
Past Tense: _____
Future Tense: _____

Keep Up The Great Work!

Activity 80 — **Unit 4** — CCSS: L.2.6, L.2.4a

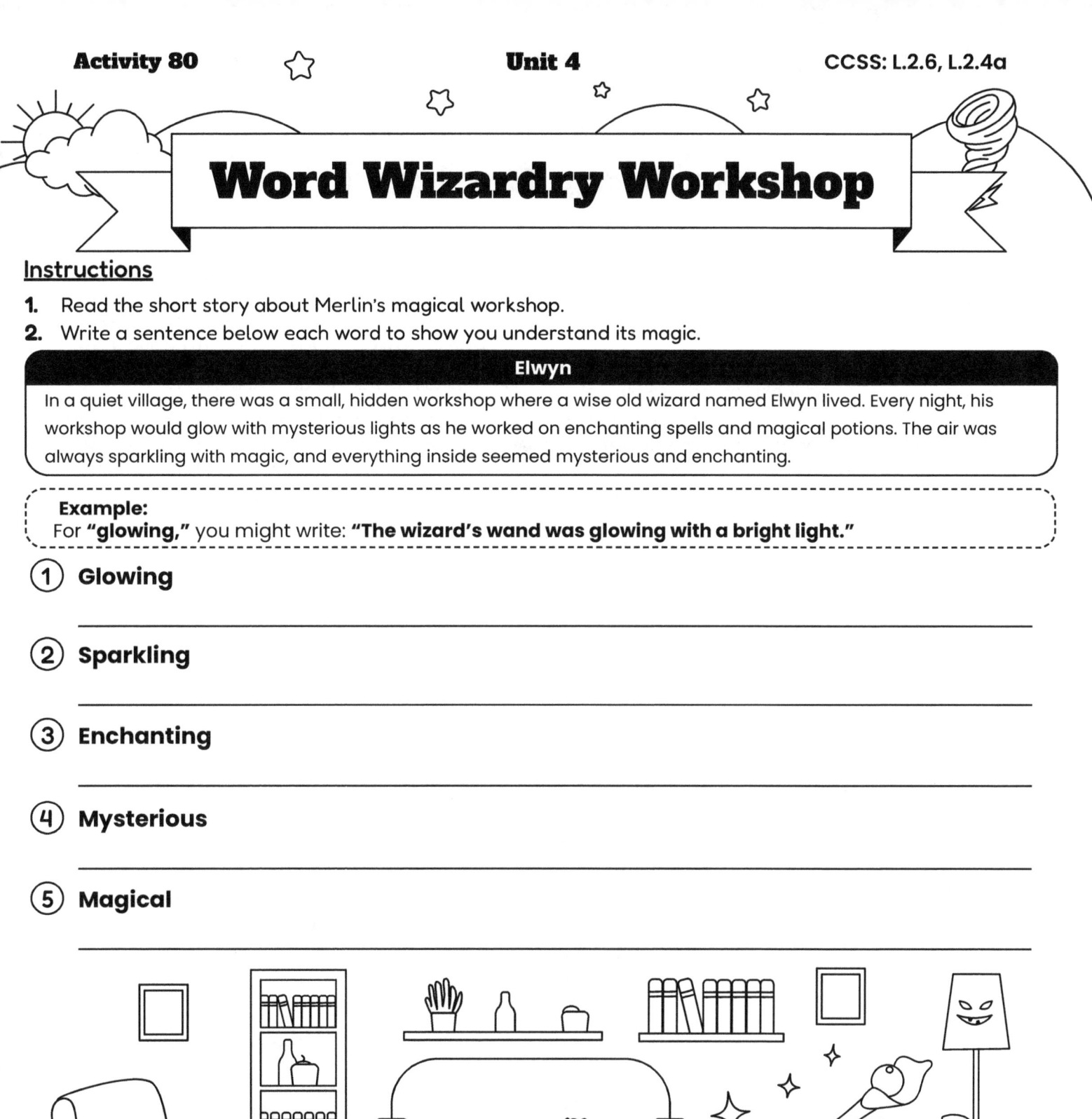

Word Wizardry Workshop

Instructions

1. Read the short story about Merlin's magical workshop.
2. Write a sentence below each word to show you understand its magic.

Elwyn

In a quiet village, there was a small, hidden workshop where a wise old wizard named Elwyn lived. Every night, his workshop would glow with mysterious lights as he worked on enchanting spells and magical potions. The air was always sparkling with magic, and everything inside seemed mysterious and enchanting.

Example:
For **"glowing,"** you might write: **"The wizard's wand was glowing with a bright light."**

① **Glowing**
_____

② **Sparkling**
_____

③ **Enchanting**
_____

④ **Mysterious**
_____

⑤ **Magical**
_____

You Are Magic!

Activity 81   **Unit 5**   CCSS: W.2.1, L.2.1f

Opinion Orchard

Instructions

1. Read the short story below to get inspired.
2. Think about your favorite fruit.
3. Write a few sentences to tell us why it's your favorite. Describe how it tastes, looks, or makes you feel.

Example:
I love grapes because they are small and sweet. Eating them makes me feel like I'm having a tiny, juicy feast. Their purple color is so pretty, and they remind me of sunny days at the park.

Visiting the Orchard

Sarah loves visiting the orchard every fall. She enjoys picking apples, tasting their sweetness, and feeling the crunch with every bite. Apples are her favorite because they remind her of fun family picnics and the cool autumn breeze.

"My favorite fruit is …"   "I like it because …"   "It tastes …"   "When I eat it, I feel …"

_____

_____

_____

_____

_____

_____

Keep it up

Activity 82   **Unit 5**   CCSS: W.2.2, W.2.7

Informative Insect Insight

Instructions
1. Read the short story below to get inspired.
2. Pick an insect that you think is interesting.
3. Use books or safe online resources to find out cool things about it.
4. Write down three fascinating facts you discover.

Incredible Ladybugs

One sunny day, Erica discovered a ladybug in her garden. She learned that ladybugs are helpful insects because they eat pests like aphids. Erica was amazed to find out that ladybugs can lay up to 1,000 eggs in their lifetime!

The insect I chose was

① **Where does this insect live?**
_____

② **What does this insect eat?**
_____

③ **What are three interesting facts about this insect?**
_____
_____
_____

Keep Exploring!

Activity 83   Unit 5   CCSS: W.2.3, L.2.2c, RI.2.1, RI.2.3

Narrative Neighbors

Instructions

1. Read the story about Buddy the golden retriever.
2. Answer the questions about the story.
3. Now, imagine a day in the life of a neighbor's pet. It could be a dog, cat, fish, or any pet.
4. Write a short story about what they do in a day.

Buddy

Buddy, the golden retriever next door, starts his day with a big stretch and a wagging tail. He loves going for a walk in the park with Mrs. Green. At the park, Buddy chases squirrels, sniffs around, and plays fetch with his favorite ball. Later, he fetches the newspaper for Mrs. Green and takes a nap. In the afternoon, Buddy helps Mrs. Green in the garden by digging holes for new plants. After a busy day, Buddy enjoys a treat and curls up in his cozy bed.

1) What activities does Buddy enjoy at the park?
_____

2) How does Buddy help Mrs. Green in the garden?
_____

3) What does Buddy do at the end of his busy day?
_____

Write a Short Story About a Neighbor's Pet

_____
_____
_____
_____

Wow! You Are A Superstar!

Activity 84 — **Unit 5** — CCSS: W.2.2, W.2.8, RI.2.1, RI.2.2

How-To Handwashing

Instructions

1. Read the story about Sarah learning to wash her hands.
2. Think about how you start washing your hands.
3. Write down each step in order, from start to finish.

Clean Hands Are Happy Hands

Sarah learned about the importance of washing her hands properly at school. Her teacher explained that washing hands helps to get rid of germs. After playing outside, Sarah came inside, turned on the tap, applied soap, and scrubbed her hands for 20 seconds. She then rinsed her hands thoroughly and dried them with a clean towel.

1) Why did Sarah wash her hands?
   _____

2) What did Sarah do after applying soap?
   _____

3) How long did Sarah scrub her hands?
   _____

STEP 1
_____
_____

STEP 2
_____
_____

STEP 3
_____
_____

STEP 4
_____
_____

STEP 5
_____
_____

Super Scrubbing!

Activity 85 — **Unit 5** — **CCSS: W.2.1, L.2.2b, RL.2.1**

Persuasive Pet Plea

Instructions

1. Read the passage about Jen persuading her parents to get a pet.
2. Answer the questions about the passage.
3. Write your own letter to your parents persuading them to get you a pet.

A New Best Friend

Jen had always wanted a pet. She loved animals and thought having a pet would be so much fun. One day, she decided to ask her parents if they could get a dog. She explained how she would take care of the dog, feed it, and walk it every day. Jen told her parents that having a dog would teach her responsibility and provide her with a loyal friend. Her parents listened carefully and promised to think about it.

1) What kind of pet did Jen want?
_____

2) How did Jen plan to take care of the dog?
_____

3) Why did Jen think having a dog would be good for her?
_____

Dear _____
_____
_____
_____
_____
_____
_____
_____

Love,
_____

Keep Up The Great Work!

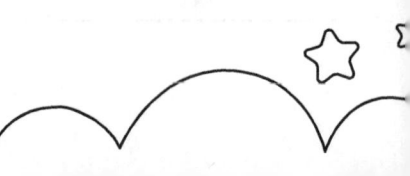

Activity 86 — **Unit 5** — CCSS: RL.2.1, W.2.3

Descriptive Dinosaur Park

Instructions
1. Read the passage about Dino World.
2. Answer the questions about the passage.

Dino World

Imagine going to Dino World, a place where dinosaurs roam freely. You see a group of velociraptors playing near a waterfall, their scales glistening in the sun. The gentle giant, an Apatosaurus, munches on leaves from the tallest trees. You hear the loud roars of a T-Rex in the distance and the chirping sounds of smaller dinosaurs nearby. The air is warm and filled with the scent of fresh rain and earth. As you walk further, you spot a triceratops family grazing in a meadow. The baby triceratops tries to imitate its mother by munching on the grass. Suddenly, a pterodactyl swoops down, its wings making a whooshing sound as it catches fish from a pond. The ground vibrates as a herd of stegosaurs marches by, their plates shining brightly.

What are the velociraptors doing near the waterfall?	What sound does the T-Rex make in the distance?	What causes the ground to vibrate?
A) Drinking water	A) Roars	A) T-Rex roaring
B) Playing	B) Growls	B) Pterodactyl flying
C) Sleeping	C) Chirps	C) Herd of stegosaurs marching

Imagine being in Dino World and write what you see, hear, and feel.

_____

_____

_____

_____

_____

Keep Exploring With Your Words!

Activity 87 — Unit 5 — CCSS: W.2.3, RL.2.1, L.2.2a

Recounting a Rainy Day

Instructions

1. Read the story about "A Rainy Day Adventure" and answer the questions about the story.
2. Then write a diary entry about your rainy day. Tell what happened, how you felt, and why it was memorable.

Rain Rain Come Again

Last Saturday, even though it was raining, I had the best day ever. My sister and I made paper boats and raced them in the stream by our house. We laughed and cheered as our boats floated down the stream. My boat won the race! Later, we jumped in puddles and splashed water everywhere. By the end of the day, we were soaked but very happy.

What did the children do with the paper boats?	How did the children feel after their boat race?	What did the children do after the boat race?
A) Threw them away B) Raced them in the stream C) Painted them	A) Sad B) Angry C) Happy	A) Went inside B) Jumped in puddles C) Took a nap

Write a diary entry about your rainy day!

_____

_____

_____

_____

You're Doing A Great Job!

Activity 88   **Unit 5**   CCSS: W.2.2, L.2.6, RI.2.1

Compare & Contrast Cookies

Instructions

1. Think of your two most favorite cookies.
2. Write down what both cookies have in common. Maybe they're both sweet or crunchy?
3. Then write how they are different. Does one have chocolate while the other has fruit?
4. Make sure to describe each cookie so someone who's never tasted them can imagine how they're alike and different.

Similarities

_____
_____
_____
_____
_____
_____
_____

Differences

_____
_____
_____
_____
_____
_____
_____

Sweet Treats

Cookies come in many flavors and textures. Sugar cookies are sweet and can be soft or crunchy. They're often decorated with icing. Peanut butter cookies are also sweet but have a nutty flavor and sometimes have peanut pieces in them. Chocolate chip cookies are popular too, with chocolate bits that melt in your mouth. Some cookies have fruit pieces, like raisins or dried cranberries, adding a chewy texture. No matter what kind, cookies are a delicious treat enjoyed by many!

What are two flavors of cookies mentioned in the passage?
A) Sugar and vanilla
B) Peanut butter and chocolate chip
C) Raisin and oatmeal

Which cookie is often decorated with icing?
A) Chocolate chip
B) Peanut butter
C) Sugar

What can be added to cookies to make them chewy?
A) Chocolate bits
B) Icing
C) Fruit pieces

Draw a picture of your two favorite cookies then color them!

Keep It Up!

Activity 89 — **Unit 5** — CCSS: W.2.3, L.2.1e, RL.2.1

My Superpower Selection

Instructions

1. Read the story about Luna and answer the questions.
2. Then write about your own superpower and how you would use it for good.

Rain Rain Come Again

Luna the Lightbringer could bring light to the darkest places. One day, Luna saw a town covered in darkness because storm clouds hid the sun. She flew over the town and used her power to light up the streets, making everyone feel safe and happy. The townspeople were grateful, and Luna felt proud to have made a difference.

What is Luna's special power?
A) Bringing light
B) Flying
C) Controlling weather

Why did Luna use her power in the town?
A) To chase away the storm clouds
B) To make everyone feel safe
C) To make the sun shine

How did the townspeople feel after Luna helped them?
A) Sad
B) Grateful
C) Angry

What superpower would you love to have?

_____
_____
_____
_____
_____
_____

How would you use your superpower for good?

_____
_____
_____
_____
_____
_____

You're A Hero In The Making!

Activity 90   **Unit 5**   CCSS: W.2.1, W.2.8

Book Review Bonanza

Instructions

1. Pick a book you've read recently.
2. Write the book's title and the author's name.
3. Answer the comprehension questions about your book.
4. Share what parts of the book you enjoyed and any parts you didn't.

Example:
I read **'Charlotte's Web.'** I loved when Wilbur made friends with the other animals, but it was sad when Charlotte got tired. It showed how friends help each other.

① Who is the main character in the book?
_____

② What is the main problem or conflict in the story?
_____

③ How is the problem or conflict resolved?
_____
_____

④ What is your favorite part of the book and why?
_____
_____

Draw a picture of your two favorite scene in the book!

Keep Exploring New Stories!

Activity 91 — **Unit 5** — CCSS: W.2.3, L.2.4a

Fantasy Field Trip

Instructions
1. Read the story about a magical field trip.
2. Answer the comprehension questions about the story.

A New Best Friend

Mrs. Willow's second-grade class went on a field trip to Fairy Forest. The trees whispered secrets and fairies danced in the air. Max, the class rabbit, led them to a hidden clearing where they found a glowing treasure chest.

1) What did the class find in the hidden clearing?
_____

Inside the chest were magical items that gave each student a special power. They used their new abilities to help the forest animals. As they walked deeper, they met an old owl named Oliver.

2) Who did the students meet in the forest, and what did they learn from him?
_____

Oliver told them about a dark spell cast over the enchanted pond. With their new powers, the children worked together to break the spell. Emily talked to the animals, Tommy controlled the water, and Lucy made plants grow. The pond sparkled back to life.

3) How did Emily, Tommy, and Lucy use their powers to help the pond?
_____

The fairies thanked the students by giving them one wish. They wished for a special treehouse where they could visit Fairy Forest anytime. A magical treehouse appeared, filled with books, games, and treasures.

4) What did the children wish for, and what was special about the treehouse?
_____

Your Imagination Is Magical!

Activity 92 — **Unit 5** — CCSS: W.2.5, L.2.2d

Poetic Seasons

Instructions

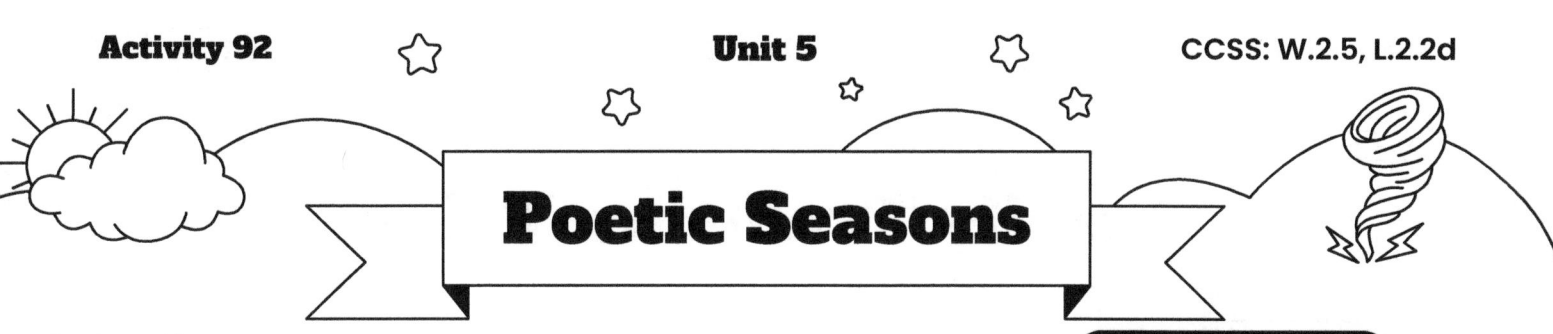

1. Read the story about the seasons below.
2. Answer the questions about the story.
3. Write a four-line poem about your favorite season.
4. In your poem, describe what you see and feel during this season.
5. Share why this season is your favorite.

Sample Poem

Winter whispers in chilly breezes,
Snowflakes dance, each one pleases.
Warm cocoa by the fire's light,
Long, cozy stories into the night.

The Magical Seasons

Once upon a time, in a magical land, there were four wonderful seasons: Spring, Summer, Autumn, and Winter. Each season had its own special charm. Spring brought blooming flowers, chirping birds, and gentle rains that made everything fresh and green. Summer was filled with long sunny days perfect for beach trips, ice cream, and playing outside until dusk. Autumn painted the trees with golden leaves, and the air was crisp and cool, making it a perfect time for cozy sweaters and hot apple cider. Winter covered the land with a blanket of snow, turning it into a wonderland where children built snowmen, went sledding, and warmed up by the fire with hot cocoa.

1. What are the four seasons mentioned in the story?
   _____

2. Which season is perfect for beach trips and playing outside until dusk?
   _____

3. What makes autumn special according to the story?
   _____

4. What activities do children enjoy in winter?
   _____

Write your four-line poem about your favorite season below

Your Poem

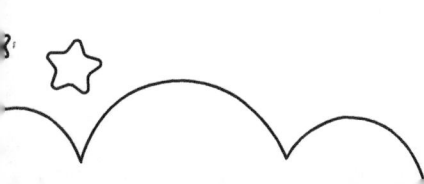

_____
_____
_____
_____
_____
_____

You're A Wonderful Poet In The Making!

Activity 93   Unit 5   CCSS: W.2.3, L.2.2a, RI.2.1

Family Tradition Tales

Instructions

1. Read the story about family traditions below.
2. Answer the fill-in-the-blank questions about the story.
3. Complete the crossword puzzle using words from the story.

Baking Cookies with Grandma

Every winter, my family has a special tradition of baking cookies with Grandma. We start by gathering all the ingredients: flour, sugar, eggs, and chocolate chips. Grandma shows us how to mix everything together, and we take turns stirring the big bowl. Once the dough is ready, we roll it into small balls and place them on a baking sheet. While the cookies bake in the oven, the kitchen fills with a delicious aroma. Finally, we sit around the table, enjoy our freshly baked cookies, and share stories. This tradition makes us all feel warm and happy.

1. In the story, the family tradition is baking _____ with Grandma.

2. They enjoy the cookies and share _____ around the table.

3. The kitchen fills with a delicious _____ while the cookies bake.

4. They gather ingredients like flour, sugar, eggs, and _____ chips.

5. This tradition makes everyone feel warm and _____ .

Keep Sharing Your Wonderful Stories!

Activity 94 **Unit 5** CCSS: W.2.5, L.2.2d

Constructing a Castle

Instructions
1. Read the story about family traditions below.
2. Answer the fill-in-the-blank questions about the story.
3. Complete the crossword puzzle using words from the story.

Sandcastle Fun

Building a sandcastle is a fun activity to enjoy at the beach. First, you need some basic tools: a bucket, a shovel, and some wet sand. Start by filling the bucket with sand and packing it down tightly. Flip the bucket over to create a solid base. Use the shovel to add details like towers and walls. Wet sand helps keep the castle sturdy. You can decorate your sandcastle with shells, stones, and seaweed. Remember to work quickly because the tide can wash your creation away!

Word Bank

shovel   stones   flip   shells   wet

1. What tools do you need to build a sandcastle?
   _____

2. Why is wet sand important for building a sandcastle?
   _____

3. How can you decorate your sandcastle?
   _____

4. What should you be careful of when building a sandcastle near the water?
   _____

Draw your dream sandcastle here

Fill-In-The-Blank

To build a sandcastle, you need a bucket, a _____, and some _____ sand.

First, fill the bucket with sand.

Then, _____ it over on the ground.

Use the _____ to add details.
You can decorate your sandcastle with _____ and _____.

Your Castle Is Coming To Life! Great Job!

Activity 95   **Unit 5**   CCSS: RL.2.1, RL.2.2, L.2.4

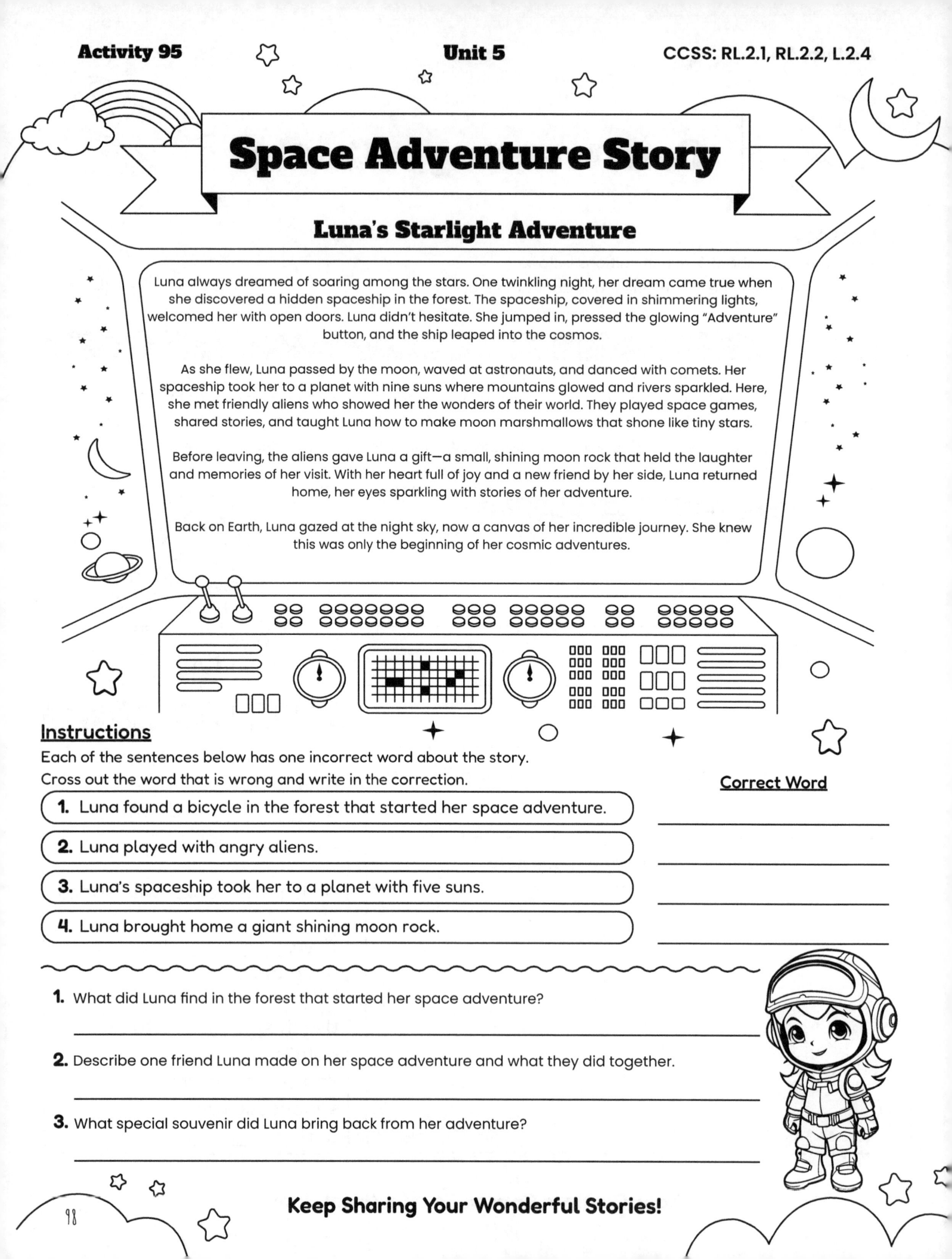

Space Adventure Story

Luna's Starlight Adventure

Luna always dreamed of soaring among the stars. One twinkling night, her dream came true when she discovered a hidden spaceship in the forest. The spaceship, covered in shimmering lights, welcomed her with open doors. Luna didn't hesitate. She jumped in, pressed the glowing "Adventure" button, and the ship leaped into the cosmos.

As she flew, Luna passed by the moon, waved at astronauts, and danced with comets. Her spaceship took her to a planet with nine suns where mountains glowed and rivers sparkled. Here, she met friendly aliens who showed her the wonders of their world. They played space games, shared stories, and taught Luna how to make moon marshmallows that shone like tiny stars.

Before leaving, the aliens gave Luna a gift—a small, shining moon rock that held the laughter and memories of her visit. With her heart full of joy and a new friend by her side, Luna returned home, her eyes sparkling with stories of her adventure.

Back on Earth, Luna gazed at the night sky, now a canvas of her incredible journey. She knew this was only the beginning of her cosmic adventures.

Instructions

Each of the sentences below has one incorrect word about the story.
Cross out the word that is wrong and write in the correction.

Correct Word

1. Luna found a bicycle in the forest that started her space adventure. _____
2. Luna played with angry aliens. _____
3. Luna's spaceship took her to a planet with five suns. _____
4. Luna brought home a giant shining moon rock. _____

---

1. What did Luna find in the forest that started her space adventure?
   _____

2. Describe one friend Luna made on her space adventure and what they did together.
   _____

3. What special souvenir did Luna bring back from her adventure?
   _____

Keep Sharing Your Wonderful Stories!

Activity 95   **Unit 5**   CCSS: W.2.3, L.2.3a, L.2.5

Instructions

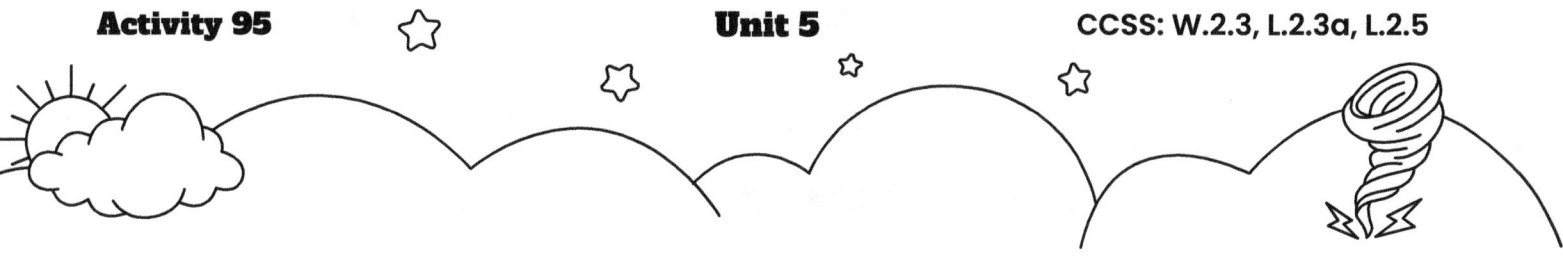

1. Imagine you are Luna and describe another adventure you would have in space.
2. Use the word bank below to help you write about a new planet you discover. What does it look like? Who lives there?
3. Describe the amazing creatures or friends you meet on this new planet.
4. What special souvenir do you bring back from this adventure? How does it remind you of your journey?

Word Bank

spaceship   planet   adventure   creatures   glowing   memories

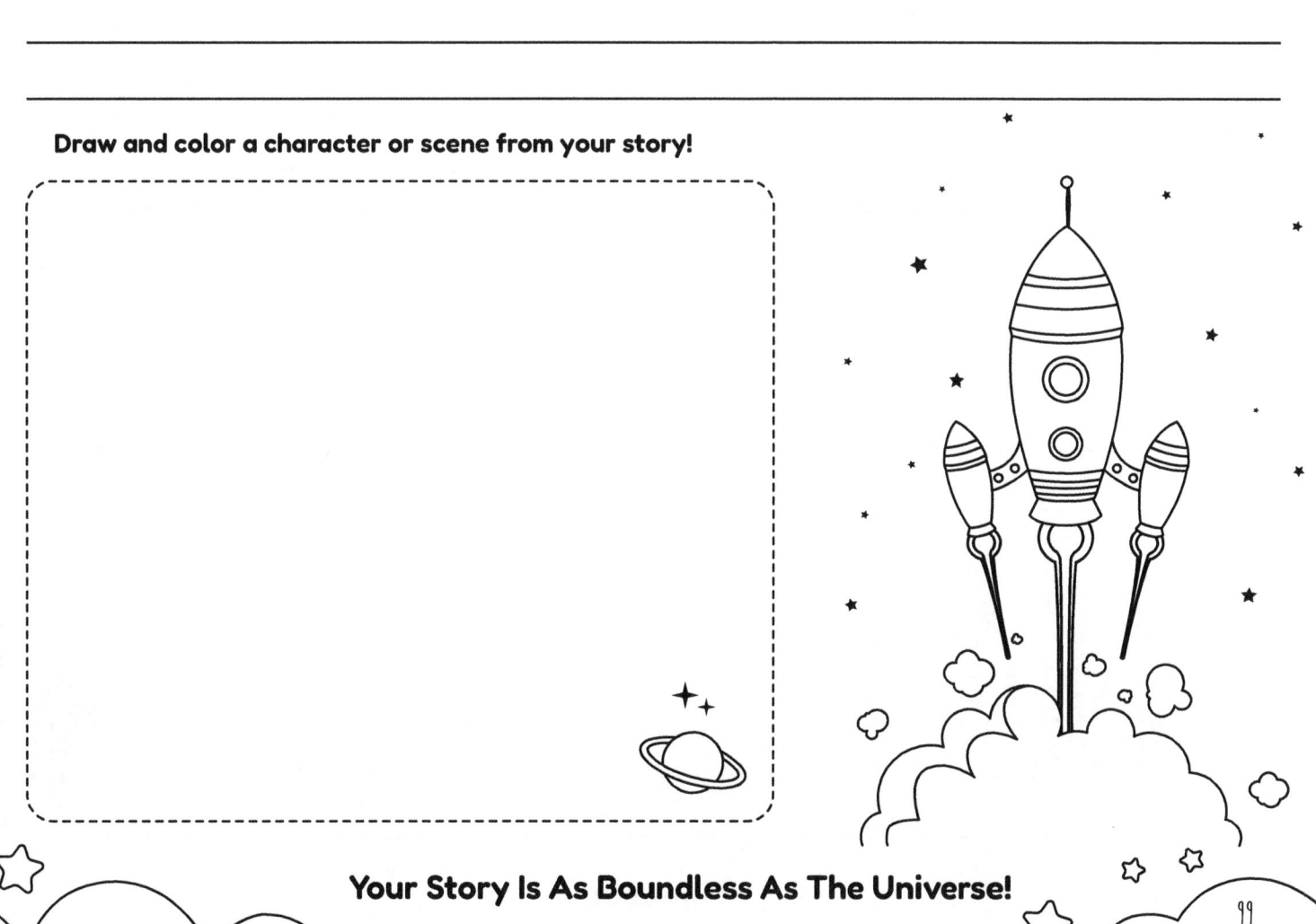

_____
_____
_____
_____
_____
_____
_____

Draw and color a character or scene from your story!

Your Story Is As Boundless As The Universe!

Activity 96   **Unit 5**   CCSS: W.2.3, W.2.8, L.2.1f, RI.2.1, RI.2.3

Gratitude Garden

Instructions
1. Read the passage about gratitude.
2. Use the diagram and write Sara's problem related to gratitude and two ways she solves it.

Finding Gratitude

Sara always thought about the things she was thankful for. One day, she realized she often took things for granted and wanted to change that. She decided to find ways to show her gratitude every day. Sara wrote thank-you notes to her family, started a gratitude journal, and helped her friends more often. This made her feel happier and more connected to the people around her.

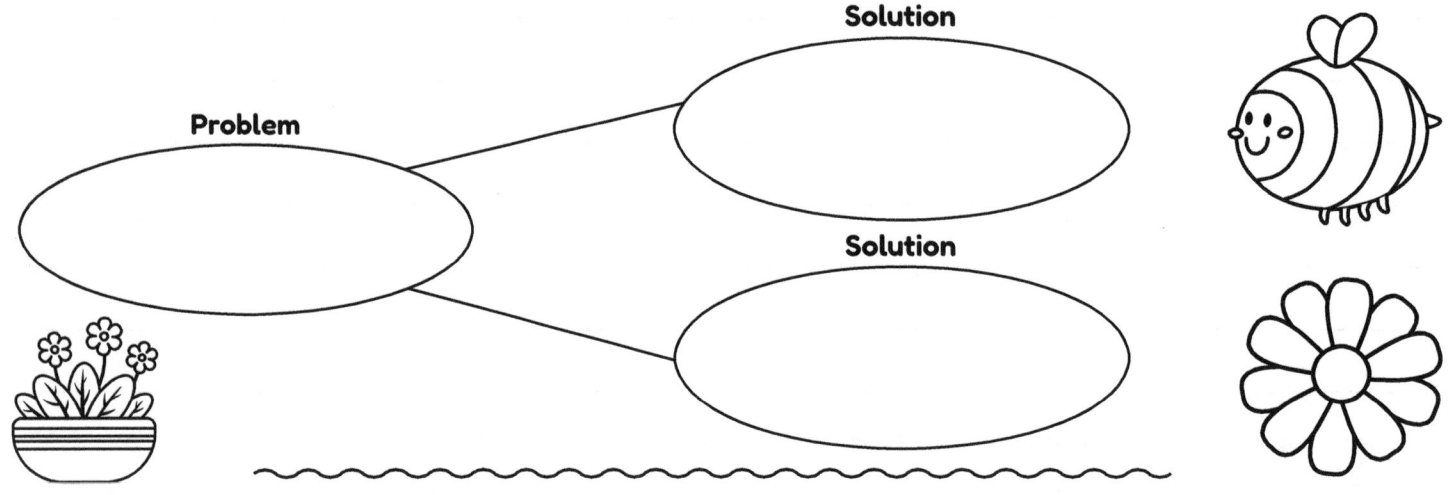

Problem → **Solution**
Problem → **Solution**

Think of three things you're thankful for then write a sentence about why each one is important to you.

1. _____
2. _____
3. _____

Draw one of the things you're thankful for

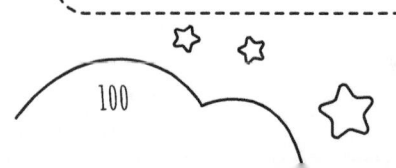

Fantastic!

Activity 97   **Unit 5**   CCSS: RI.2.1, L.2.4a

Mystery in the Museum

Instructions

1. Read the passage about Ben, the night guard, and the moving toys.
2. Fill in the missing words in the story using the word shapes provided.

Sunnyville Toy Museum

One night, Ben, a new night guard at the Sunnyville Toy Museum, was ready for his shift. The museum had all sorts of toys: fluffy teddy bears, shiny toy trains, and even colorful puzzles. Everything looked so still and quiet.

As Ben walked around, he heard a soft thump. He turned around but saw nothing. "It must be my imagination," he thought. He continued his rounds, checking each room carefully.

When Ben returned to the main hall, he noticed something strange. The _____ bear that was sitting on a small chair was now on the floor! And the toy _____ seemed to have moved too.

Ben was puzzled. "How did these toys _____?" he wondered. He decided to sit quietly and watch. As the clock struck _____, he couldn't believe his eyes. The toys began to move all by themselves! The teddy bear climbed back onto the chair, and the toy trains _____ along their tracks.

Ben realized that the toys come to _____ at night. He smiled and decided to keep their secret. From that night on, Ben looked forward to his shifts, watching the toys' midnight adventures.

Word Bank

move   trains   chugged   midnight   teddy   life

① ② ③ ④ ⑤ ⑥

You Did a Terrific Job!

Dream Destination

Mystical Island

Once upon a time, in a world of magic and wonder, there was an island where everything was different. This island was not like any place you've seen before. It had trees with leaves in all the colors of the rainbow, and flowers that could sing when the wind blew.

The animals on this island were very friendly. There were talking rabbits, dancing monkeys, and even a giant turtle that could carry people on its back. The sky was a bright blue, and sometimes at night, it changed to purple and pink.

In the middle of the island, there was a crystal-clear lake. The water in the lake was so clean and shiny that it looked like liquid diamonds. People said that swimming in this lake made you feel happy and full of energy.

The most amazing thing about this island was the candy waterfall. Yes, a waterfall made of candy! It had streams of chocolate, caramel, and even rainbow-colored candies. Visitors could catch the candies in little buckets and eat them.

This magical island was a place of happiness, adventure, and wonder. It was a dream destination for anyone who loved magic and fun.

Great Job!

Activity 98   **Unit 5**   CCSS: W.2.3, L.2.5a

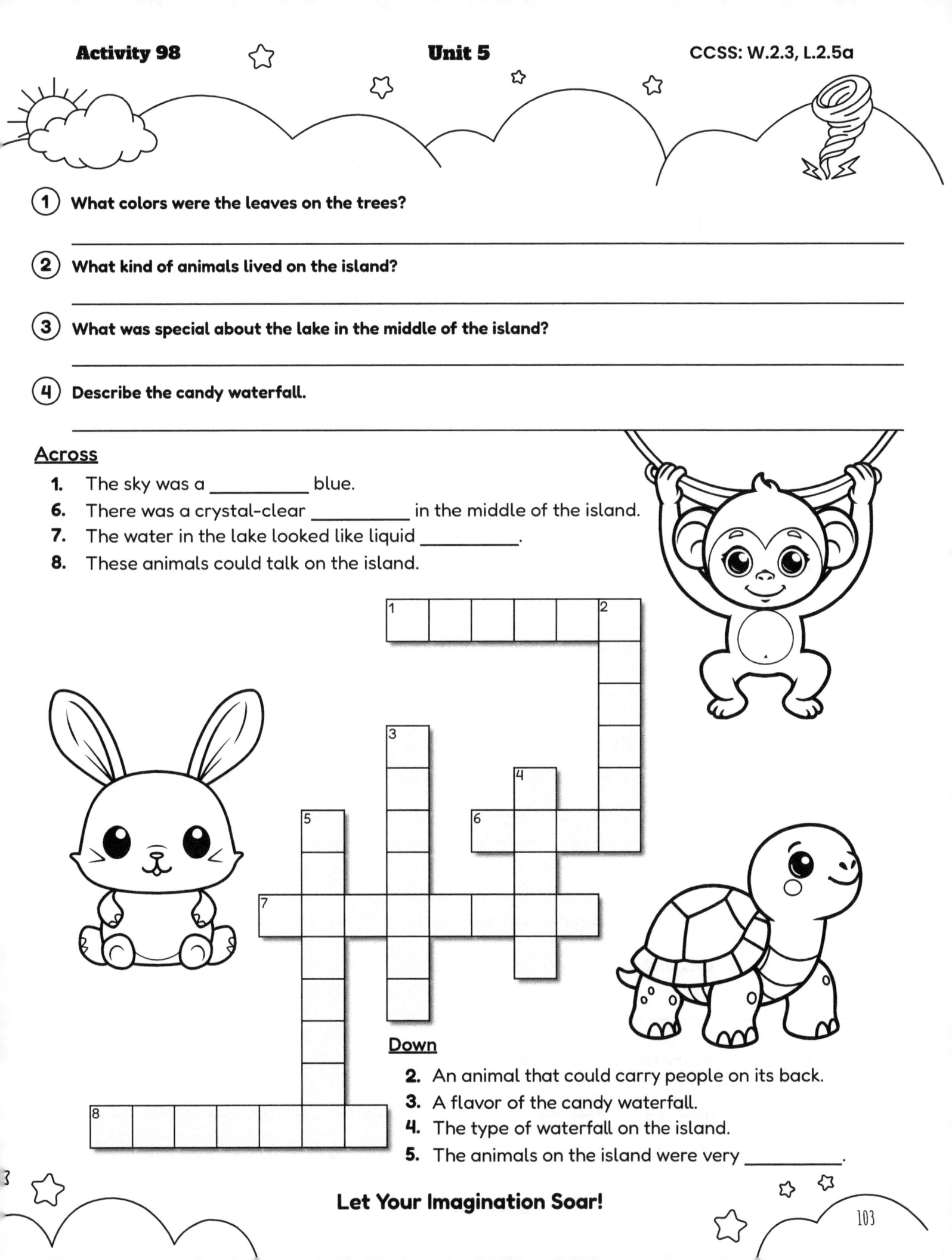

1) What colors were the leaves on the trees?
_____

2) What kind of animals lived on the island?
_____

3) What was special about the lake in the middle of the island?
_____

4) Describe the candy waterfall.
_____

Across
1. The sky was a _____ blue.
6. There was a crystal-clear _____ in the middle of the island.
7. The water in the lake looked like liquid _____.
8. These animals could talk on the island.

Down
2. An animal that could carry people on its back.
3. A flavor of the candy waterfall.
4. The type of waterfall on the island.
5. The animals on the island were very _____.

Let Your Imagination Soar!

Activity 99 — **Unit 5** — CCSS: RI.2.1, RI.2.3, RI.2.5

My Future Invention

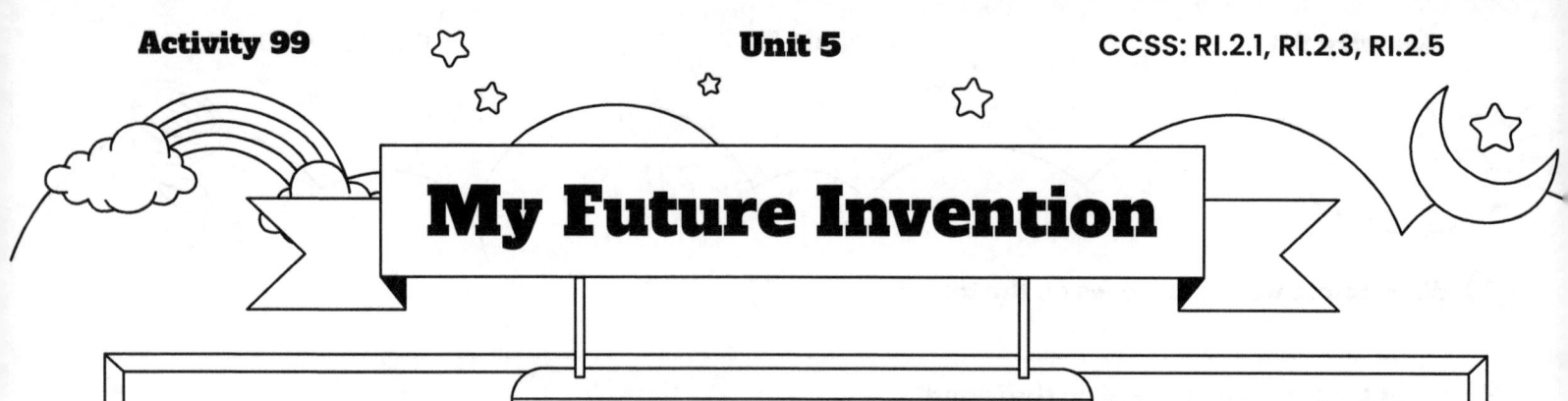

The Helping Hands Gadget

In the small town of Sunnyville, there was a second grader named Jamie who loved to invent things. One day, Jamie thought of a brilliant idea for a new invention. It was called the "Helping Hands Gadget." This gadget was not just any ordinary device; it was special.

The Helping Hands Gadget was a small, robot-like machine with many arms. Each arm could do different things. One could pick up toys, another could help water plants, and another could even help with homework!

Jamie worked very hard, using cardboard, some old toy parts, and a lot of imagination. Finally, the gadget was ready. It was painted bright yellow and had big friendly eyes. Jamie showed the invention to friends and family, who were all amazed by how helpful it was.

The best part about the Helping Hands Gadget was that it made life easier for everyone. Parents loved it because it could clean up rooms quickly. Kids loved it because it could play games with them. Even pets loved it because one of its arms could gently pet them.

Jamie felt proud and happy, knowing that the invention brought joy and help to many people.

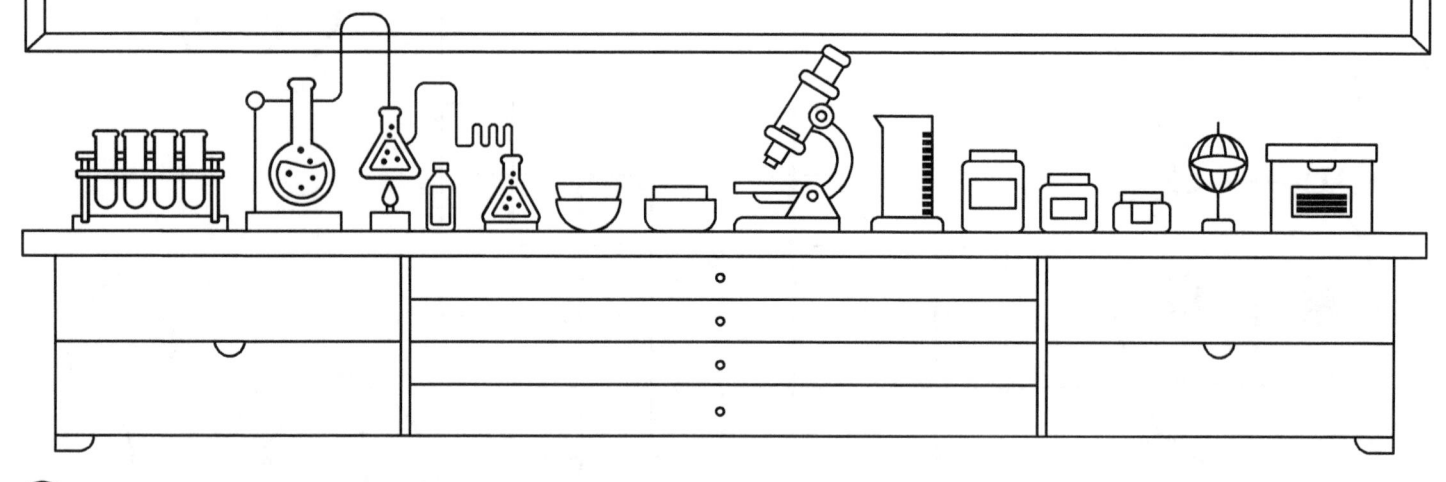

1. Why did parents, kids, and pets love the Helping Hands Gadget?

   _____

2. How did Jamie build the Helping Hands Gadget?

   _____

Fantastic Job!

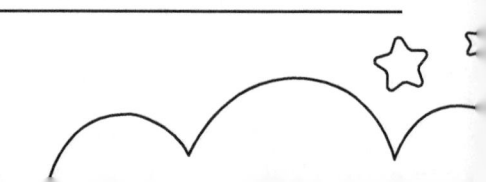

Activity 99   **Unit 5**   CCSS: W.2.3, L.2.1e

Instructions

1. Read the story about Jamie and the "Helping Hands Gadget.
2. Fill in the chart below with information from the story.

Feature	Description
Name of the Invention	
What it Can Do	
Materials Used	
Impact on People and Pets	

Draw and color a picture of your own invention!

Let Your Imagination Soar!

Activity 100 — Unit 5 — CCSS: RI.2.1, RI.2.6, W.2.2, W.2.7

Animal Adaptation Article

Instructions

1. Read the passage about the arctic fox.
2. Fill in the blanks with the correct facts then answer the questions below.

The Arctic Fox

In the freezing Arctic, where temperatures can drop very low, there's a special animal called the arctic fox. These animals have amazing adaptations that help them survive in the cold!

The arctic fox has thick fur that keeps it warm. Its fur is like a thick coat that helps keep the cold out and the warmth in. In the winter, the arctic fox's fur turns white, blending in with the snow. This helps it stay hidden from predators and sneak up on prey.

Arctic foxes can survive in temperatures as low as _____.

The arctic fox is small and has a compact body shape, which helps it conserve heat. Its short legs, ears, and snout reduce heat loss. Arctic foxes also have keen hearing that allows them to locate prey under the snow.

They have fur on their paws, which helps them walk on snow and ice without getting cold.

During the summer, arctic foxes shed their white fur for a _____ coat, which helps them blend in with the tundra's rocky landscape.

① What helps the arctic fox stay warm?
_____

② Why does the arctic fox's fur change color in winter?
_____

③ How does the arctic fox's body shape help it survive the cold?
_____

④ What special feature do the arctic fox's paws have?
_____

Did You Know?

① Arctic foxes can survive in temperatures as low as -58°F (-50°C).

② They have great hearing that allows them to locate prey under the snow.

③ During the summer, arctic foxes shed their white fur for a brown or gray coat, which helps them blend in with the tundra's rocky landscape.

Draw a picture of an arctic fox showing one of its special adaptations

You Are So Talented!

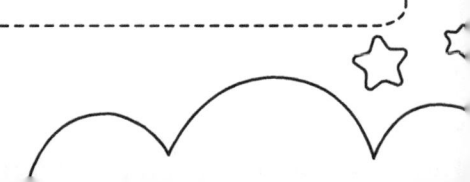

10 EXCITING STORIES FOR Second Grade

INCLUDES AUDIO BONUS

SCAN ME

Common Core Standards

Unit 1: Phonics and Word Recognition

RF.2.3: Know and apply grade-level phonics and word analysis skills in decoding words.
- **RF.2.3a:** Distinguish long and short vowels in one-syllable words.
- **RF.2.3b:** Know spelling-sound correspondences for common vowel teams.
- **RF.2.3c:** Decode regularly spelled two-syllable words with long vowels.
- **RF.2.3d:** Decode words with common prefixes and suffixes.
- **RF.2.3e:** Identify words with inconsistent but common spelling-sound correspondences.

Unit 2: Reading Fluency

RF.2.4: Read with sufficient accuracy and fluency to support comprehension.
- **RF.2.3a:** Distinguish long and short vowels in one-syllable words.
- **RF.2.3b:** Know spelling-sound correspondences for common vowel teams.
- **RF.2.3c:** Decode regularly spelled two-syllable words with long vowels.

Unit 3: Informational Text

- **RI.2.1:** Ask and answer questions about key details in a text.
- **RI.2.2:** Identify the main topic and retell key details of a text.
- **RI.2.3:** Describe the connection between historical events, scientific ideas, or steps in technical procedures.
- **RI.2.4:** Determine the meaning of words and phrases in a text.
- **RI.2.5:** Know and use text features to locate key facts or information.
- **RI.2.6:** Identify the main purpose of a text.
- **RI.2.7:** Explain how images contribute to and clarify a text.
- **RI.2.8:** Describe how reasons support specific points the author makes.
- **RI.2.9:** Compare and contrast the most important points in two texts on the same topic.
- **RI.2.10:** Read and comprehend informational texts proficiently.

Unit 4: Literature

- **RL.2.1:** Ask and answer questions about key details in a text.
- **RL.2.2:** Recount stories and determine their central message, lesson, or moral.
- **RI.2.3:** Describe how characters respond to major events and challenges.
- **RL.2.4:** Describe how words and phrases supply rhythm and meaning in a story, poem, or song.
- **RL.2.5:** Describe the overall structure of a story.
- **RL.2.6:** Acknowledge differences in characters' points of view.
- **RL.2.7:** Use information from illustrations and words to understand characters, setting, or plot.
- **RL.2.8:** Describe how reasons support specific points the author makes.
- **RL.2.9:** Compare and contrast two or more versions of the same story.
- **RL.2.10:** Read and comprehend literature proficiently.

Unit 5: Vocabulary and Language

- **L.2.1:** Ask and answer questions about key details in a text.
- **L.2.2:** Recount stories and determine their central message, lesson, or moral.
- **L.2.3:** Describe how characters respond to major events and challenges.
- **L.2.4:** Describe how words and phrases supply rhythm and meaning in a story, poem, or song.
- **L.2.5:** Describe the overall structure of a story.
- **L.2.6:** Acknowledge differences in characters' points of view.

Could you spare just a minute?

Our biggest joy comes from helping little ones flourish and discover the world around them through learning.

That's why your thoughts matter so much to us!

Your honest thoughts about our book, even a quick sentence or two, would mean the world. We really mean it!

You'd be making a big difference for a small education brand like ours, run with love by a mother-daughter team.

Your reviews help us reach more curious minds across the globe, paving their way to success in their educational journey.

And hey, maybe we'll even sell a few more books in the process!

Every single review makes our hearts swell with gratitude.

Ready to make our day?

Scan the QR Code below to share your thoughts.